DRIVING SKILLS

David Lambert
and
The Diagram Group

HarperCollins*Publishers*

HarperCollins Publishers
P.O. Box, Glasgow G4 0NB

A Diagram book first created by Diagram Visual Information
Limited of 195 Kentish Town Road, London NW5 8SY

First published 1995

Reprint 10 9 8 7 6 5 4 3 2 1 0

Crown copyright material from the Highway Code is reproduced
with the permission of the Controller of HMSO

ISBN 0 00 470736 2

A catalogue record for this book is available
from the British Library

Printed in Hong Kong

Introduction

Learning to drive requires both memorizing the Highway Code's regulations for motorists and clocking up hours of on-the-road practice with a driving instructor. *Collins Pocket Reference Driving Skills* is the perfect guide for learners, combining in one volume essential information to help you learn to drive, pass the driving test, and maintain your vehicle.

Collins Pocket Reference Driving Skills puts you in the driver's seat with step-by-step practice exercises and reminders of Highway Code regulations governing each manoeuvre. From moving away from the kerb, to motorway driving, to dealing with breakdowns and accidents – every type of road situation is covered in clear language with accompanying diagrams.

You'll also find out how to apply to take your driving test when you're ready. The official syllabus of the driving test is provided, as well as a detailed overview of each part of the test: what the examiner looks for, what skills you will be tested on, what to avoid.

You'll also discover what you need to do after passing your test: how to read your licence, and how to insure and secure your own car and have it MOT tested. Finally, detailed text and diagrams about vehicle anatomy help you to understand how a car works and what may be involved when yours needs servicing or repair. Important car and driving terms used in the book are defined in the comprehensive glossary.

Contents

3: ON THE ROAD

4: SPECIAL SITUATIONS

5: THE DRIVING TEST

6: AFTER THE TEST

7: CAR SYSTEMS

1. In the driving seat

This chapter describes the main controls in a car –
where they are, what they look like, what they are for,
how to use them, and what to avoid. Most cars have a
similar layout of major hand- and foot-operated
controls, though switches and indicators vary more in
design and location. The focus is on cars with manual
gear change. Learners who pass a driving test on a car
with automatic transmission are only qualified to drive
cars with automatic gears; learning on a car with
manual gears qualifies you to drive both types.
Familiarize yourself with the controls before you first
start to drive; get used to placing your hand or foot on
each control without having to take your eye off the
road. This chapter also gives advice on maintaining a
car and detecting common defects.

CAR SYSTEMS: AN OVERVIEW

A car is a complex piece of machinery. The driving test
does not require you to know how it all works, but you
will be expected to have some knowledge of basic
maintenance (e.g. checking radiator water level, battery,
oil and tyres). In future, the written test may require
some knowledge about the engine. In any case, it is
useful to be familiar with the main systems. For more
detailed information on car systems, see Chapter 7.
1 The car body and frame may be assembled as one
unit, or the body may be attached to a supporting
'skeleton' known as the chassis.

2 The engine contains spark plugs and pistons that move to and fro in cylinders, providing the energy to spin the wheels, charge the battery and, in many cars, to assist braking and steering.

3 The electric system starts the engine and keeps it running, as well as operating instruments, lights, horn and radio. Key items are the battery, starter motor, coil and distributor.

The cooling system employs cool air or water to stop the engine overheating. In water-cooled engines a pump sends water from a fan-cooled radiator through a jacket surrounding the cylinders and back to the radiator. In air-cooled systems air from a fan cools the engine.

4 The fuel system in most cars has a fuel pump that drives fuel from the petrol tank through a filter to the carburettor where the petrol or diesel fuel mixes with air so it will burn. Cars without a carburettor have a fuel injection system instead. (Piston movements let the fuel-air mixture into the engine's cylinders, where spark plugs ignite the mixture which then explodes, keeping the pistons moving.)

5 The transmission system converts the pistons' to-and-fro motion to rotary motion and transmits this to the wheels via a revolving drive shaft and the meshing toothed wheels called gears housed in a gearbox.

The lubrication system protects the engine's moving parts against friction damage by means of an oil pump which feeds these components oil from the crank case.

6 The steering system turns the front wheels by means of a linkage assembly, gears and a steering column controlled by the driver's steering wheel.

Most wheels are of steel, held in place by wheel nuts concealed by a detachable hub cap, and supporting inflated synthetic rubber tyres.

7 The braking system involves so-called drum brakes or disc brakes. Pushing down the foot brake causes fluid to flow from a master cylinder to the wheels' brake cylinders. The resulting hydraulic pressure produces friction which slows down the wheels.

8 The emission control system in modern cars includes a catalytic converter and other devices to reduce the amount of pollutant waste gases emitted from the engine via the exhaust pipe.

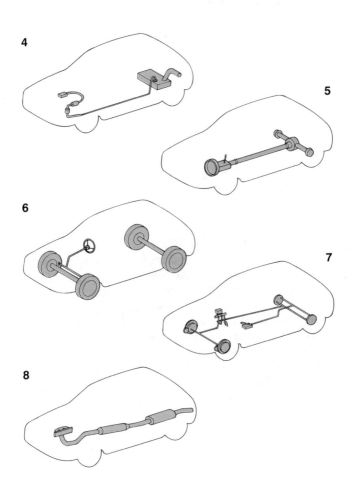

4

5

6

7

8

9 The suspension system employs springs and shock absorbers. These smooth out the effects of bumps in the road and stop a car bouncing up and down uncontrollably. The suspension system gives a smooth ride and reduces wear on components.

9

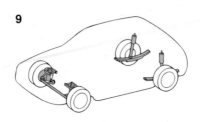

SITTING COMFORTABLY

- Make sure you have a comfortable sitting position that gives you a good view both of the instrument panel and through the windscreen and lets you easily reach the controls described subsequently.
- You can adjust a driving seat to move forward or backward (**a**), with its back upright or tilted (**b**). In some vehicles the seat can be raised or lowered (**c**). You should also be able to adjust the seat's head restraint (**d**) to support your head and neck safely in case of a severe shunting accident.
- Making sure the handbrake is on, slide the seat forward or backward until you can sit with your left foot pressing the clutch pedal with your knee slightly bent.

- Make sure you can hold the steering wheel lightly without your arms feeling stretched or restricted.
- If the steering wheel seems too high or too low you might be able to tilt the steering column up or down a bit, though not on all vehicles. If you adjust the steering column, be sure you can still see the instrument panel. Lock the steering column in place after any adjustment.
- After making these adjustments check that you have a good view of the road in front.

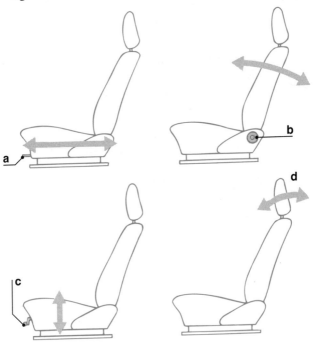

STEERING WHEEL
● The wheel in front of the driver's seat.

Purpose
● To turn the car's front wheels left or right to change direction. Many vehicles have power-assisted steering (PAS), reducing the effort required.

Control
● Normally with both hands placed on the wheel in a 'ten-to-two' (ten minutes to two o'clock) (**a**) or 'quarter-to-three' position.
● For turning techniques see pp.47–8.

Avoid
● Taking both hands off the steering wheel while driving.
● Crossing hands when you turn.
● Turning the wheel of a stationary vehicle. This could damage the steering mechanism and tyres.

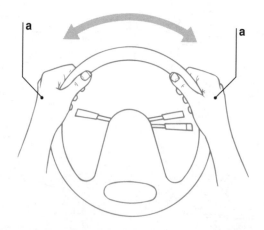

ACCELERATOR PEDAL
- The right-hand foot pedal (**a**).

Purpose
- To boost the flow of fuel to the engine to increase its speed and power.

Control
- Pushing down the right-hand foot pedal with the ball of your right foot, while your heel rests on the floor. For details see pp.43–6.

Avoid
- Pushing down too little.
- Pushing down too much.
- Pushing down jerkily.

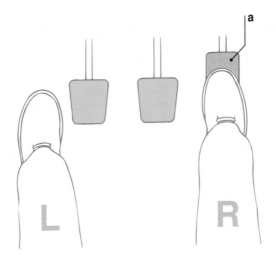

FOOT BRAKE
- The middle foot pedal (**b**).

Purpose
- To slow or stop a vehicle. In many vehicles the brake pedal gives controlled braking on all wheels.

Control
- Pushing down the foot brake with the ball of your right foot, increasing pressure progressively.

Avoid
- Stamping hard on the foot brake, so locking the wheels and making the car skid.

CLUTCH PEDAL
- The left-hand foot pedal (**c**).

Purpose
- To disengage the engine from the road wheels while you change from one gear to another, then re-engage engine and wheels once the gear change is made.

Control
- Pushing down the clutch pedal with the ball of your left foot disengages the engine by separating a clutch plate linked to the wheels from a clutch plate linked to the engine. This second plate revolves all the time; the first plate revolves only when both plates engage. Gradually releasing the clutch pedal re-engages both plates. When you reach this 'biting point' there is a slight drop in the speed and pitch of the engine.

Avoid
- Lifting your foot off the clutch pedal while still changing gear.
- Lifting your foot suddenly, so stalling the engine or making your vehicle suddenly jerk forward.

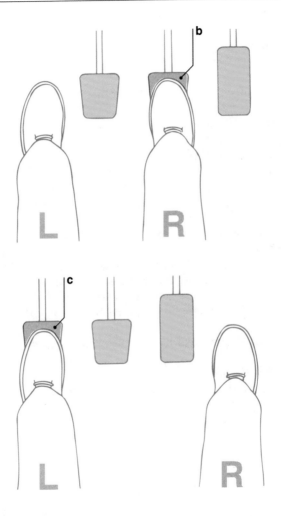

GEAR LEVER

- Usually the front of two floor-mounted levers (**1**) left of the driver's seat. On some cars it projects from the steering column or instrument panel.

Purpose

- To change from one gear to another so that the engine speed and road speed match.

Control

- With the clutch pedal down, use your left hand to move the gear lever left or right and up or down to change from one gear to another.
- A gear lever has seven (**a**) or six (**b, c**) positions: neutral (**d**) (with no gear engaged), four or five forward gears, and one position for reverse gear. The driver starts forward in first gear, and works up through the gears as the vehicle picks up speed. On a typical five-gear lever (**a**), this means tracing out the shape of an H, with the fifth forward gear and reverse gear traced out as a sideways T to the right of the H. Some cars, though, have reverse to the left (**c**).

Avoid

- Looking at the gear lever while changing gear.

HANDBRAKE

- Usually the rear floor-mounted lever (**2**) left of the driver, but below the instrument panel in some cars.

Purpose

- To keep a vehicle stationary once it has stopped, as at traffic lights, at a road junction or to park.

Control

- To apply the handbrake, grasp it with the left hand, pushing down the button at the end of the lever (**e**)

with your thumb. With the button pushed down, pull
the lever up as far as it goes. Then release the button
and lever.

● To release a handbrake reverse this procedure.

Avoid

● Applying the handbrake without pushing down its
  button. This damages the ratchet mechanism.
● Applying the handbrake in a moving vehicle unless
  the foot brake fails. You might make the car skid.

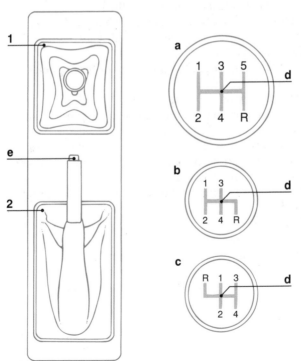

REAR-VIEW MIRRORS

- An interior mirror between driver and windscreen (**a**) and one side mirror on each door (**b**) and (**c**).

Routine checks

- Before setting off, a driver should clean and adjust all three mirrors (after adjusting seat) to give the best views of the road behind as seen from the driving position.

Use

- Before opening a car door from the inside.
- Before moving off. But also turn your head to the right to look back at the blind spots that are obstructed.
- Before signalling.
- Before overtaking, changing lanes or turning left or right.
- Before slowing down or stopping.
- When approaching a situation where you might need to overtake, turn, speed up or slow down.
- While driving along to assess what is behind. Use mirrors often for this. Fast motorway driving calls for even more frequent use.
- In anti-glare position when driving in traffic at night.

Avoid

- Driving with dirty, misted, iced-up, broken or misaligned mirrors.
- Adjusting mirrors in a moving vehicle.
- Relying on mirrors to show you road users hidden in your vehicle's blind spots (**d**). Turn your head right and look back before setting off. Glance briefly sideways before joining a dual carriageway, changing lanes, moving from lane to lane where traffic merges from left or right, or to locate a following vehicle that

has disappeared from your mirrors. Note, however,
that looking round can cause swerving at high speeds.
Use your mirrors constantly to maintain awareness of
other vehicles on the road.

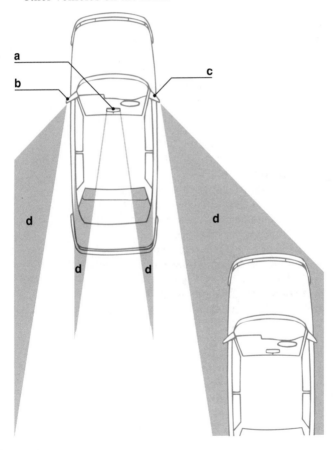

INSTRUMENT PANEL

This panel faces the driver. In your driving test you will
be expected to know what its gauges and warning lights
represent. Their layout varies from car to car. Each
car's handbook should give detailed information. The
following list includes items not found in all cars:

- A calibrated fuel gauge (**a**) indicating whether the
fuel tank is full, three-quarters full, half full, one-
quarter full, or empty. A warning light may come on
if the fuel level gets dangerously low.
- A speedometer (**b**) showing current speed with an
odometer giving total and journey mileage.
- Direction indicator warning lights (**c**), usually
accompanied by ticking or another warning sound.
- A headlight main (high) beam indicator light. This is
usually blue (**d**).
- A temperature gauge or warning light, which
indicates if the engine is overheating (**e**).
- A rev counter showing engine speed in rpm
(revolutions per minute).
- An oil-pressure warning light (**f**).
- An ignition warning light indicating low battery or
alternator charge (**g**).
- A warning light showing the handbrake is on (**h**).
- A warning light showing a worn brake pad (**i**).
- A warning light for low brake fluid level (**j**).
- A seat-belt warning light (**k**).
- A warning light showing an open door.
- A warning light showing an unsecured boot.
- A warning light showing the rear fog lamp is on (**l**).
- Hazard-light control/warning light (**m**).
- An indicator light for the rear window heater (**n**).
- Indicators for headlamps, side lights and fog lights.

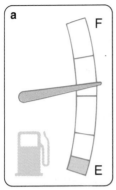

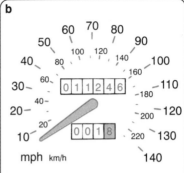

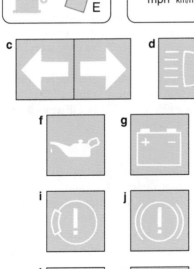

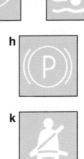

DIRECTION INDICATORS

- Winking lights on a car's front and rear offside and nearside. In many cars these are controlled by a stalk projecting from the right (**a**) or left (**b**) of the steering column (check your car handbook for location if it differs).

Purpose

- To show other road users that you intend moving or turning to the right or left.

Control

- Gently push the indicator stalk in the direction that you will be turning the steering wheel. This applies whichever side the stalk is on. Returning the stalk to the horizontal position switches off the indicators.

Avoid

- Making unnecessary or confusing signals or leaving indicators switched on after turning right or left. Most indicators are self-cancelling, but do not always turn off if your change of direction was slight.

HORN

- A device producing a loud warning sound, located on a pad or pads on the steering wheel (**c**) and/or on the tip of the stalk controlling the direction indicators (**d**).

Purpose

- To warn other road users you are there, for instance at a bend in a narrow lane, or when wanting to overtake a slow vehicle blocking your path.

Control

- Pressing the horn pad firmly once to produce a warning sound, then releasing.

Avoid

- Loud, pugnacious hooting.
- Startling other road users.
- Sounding the horn when stationary unless a moving vehicle endangers your own.
- Sounding the horn in built-up areas between 11.30 pm and 7 am except as above.

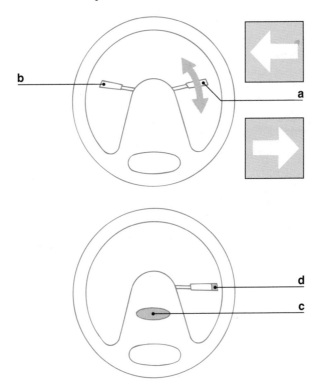

LIGHTS AND LIGHTING CONTROLS

Headlamps and side lights

- The headlamps (also called 'headlights') (**a**) are two big, bright lamps on the front wings, designed to help you see and be seen in poor light. They operate on main or dipped beam. Flashing headlamps day or night signal a warning, like sounding the horn.
- Side lights (**b**) and rear lights are small, dim lamps on front and rear. When switched on, they help people to see stationary cars at night or in dim daylight.
- Headlamp and sidelight controls usually lie on a stalk that sprouts from the steering column, with three positions: off; side, rear and numberplate lights on; and all lights on (with control for dipping). A blue warning light on the instrument panel may show when headlamps are on main beam. (See pp.22–3.)

Brake lights

These red rear lights (**c**) come on automatically if a driver applies the foot brake. They warn following traffic that the vehicle ahead is slowing down.

Hazard warning lights

These are orange flashing front, rear and side lights (**d**) used to warn other drivers that your vehicle forms an obstruction, for instance if it breaks down and is blocking part of the road. The hazard warning light switch is shown as a triangle on the instrument panel. (See also pp.22–3.)

Reversing lights

These are rear lamps that come on automatically when a vehicle reverses (**e**). They help the driver to see when backing at night or in a dark space, and to alert others.

Fog lamps

These lamps (**f**) are used with the headlights and rear
lights in bad weather. The fog lamp switch tends to be
on the instrument panel. (See also pp.22–3.)

Front of car

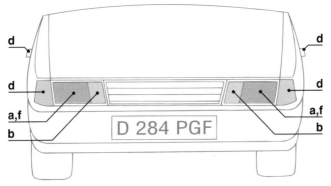

Rear of car

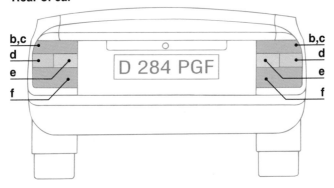

WINDSCREEN WIPERS

● Metal rods bearing rubber blades that sweep to and fro on the windscreen and, in some cars, the rear window. Washers squirt water stored in bottles through nozzles onto the windscreen and, in some cars, the rear window, to help the wipers to work.

Purpose

● To prevent mud, dust, grime, rain, snow or sleet impairing your vision.

Control

● Windscreen washer and wiper controls are normally on a stalk on the steering column (**a**). If present, rear window wiper and washer controls are separate.

Avoid

● Taking your eyes off the road to switch on a washer and wiper. If your hands are at the proper positions on the steering wheel, you should be able to operate the switch with your fingertips. Learn to do this without looking at the controls.

● Cleaning windows with dry wiper blades. This might scratch the glass.

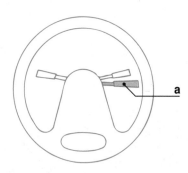

- Worn wiper blades. Replace blades if necessary.
- Empty washer bottles. Regularly check the water level and refill bottles when they are low. Additives improve effectiveness and prevent windows icing up when washed in cold weather.
- Letting wiper blades and windscreen get dirty. Wash both often with a sponge dipped in water.

WINDOW HEATING
Purpose
- To stop condensation obscuring your view through windscreen and rear window in cold, wet conditions.
- To stop ice forming on windows.
Controls
- Most cars have, on the instrument panel, a pressure pad (**a**) which lights up when pressed, switching on an electric rear-window heater.
- Some cars have another pad (**b**) operating a windscreen heater. When the engine is warmed up, this will direct hot air from the car's heater to demist the windscreen, and sometimes also the front side windows. Setting the fan control to maximum produces the strongest effect.

IGNITION SWITCH AND STARTER
- A lock in the side of the steering column.

Purpose
- To operate electrical equipment and start the engine.

Control
- Inserting an ignition key in the lock in the steering column (**a**) and turning the key clockwise to one of three positions (1–3):
  - Position **1** turns on the radio and some other electrical equipment. (Note that side lights and on many cars headlights work with the ignition switched off. Leaving headlights on with the engine off runs down the car battery, and the car may not then start.)
  - Position **2** switches on the instrument panel, gauges and ignition. A red warning light may come on.
  - Position **3** activates the starter and direction indicators. (See p.41 for how to operate.)
- The handbrake must be on and the gear lever in neutral before the ignition key is turned on.
- If an anti-theft device locks the steering column, turning the ignition key might be impossible without first slightly turning the steering wheel.

Avoid
- Keeping the ignition key turned once the engine starts. This could harm the starter motor.

CHOKE
- A pull-out stop below or on the instrument panel. In cars with an automatic choke, there is no mechanism to operate (though its setting can be permanently adjusted to make the engine run faster or slower). A

warning light (**b**) shows when a manual choke is on.

Purpose
- To cut down the amount of air in the air/fuel mixture to make a cold petrol engine easy to start.

Control
- Pull the choke mechanism out before turning the ignition key.
- Once the engine is running, push the choke steadily in before the engine starts to make a heavy chugging sound. (See also p.41.)

Avoid
- Leaving the choke fully out too long after starting the engine. This can flood the engine with fuel, making it stall.
- Leaving a choke partly out after the engine warms up. This wastes fuel, could damage the engine, and might set in motion a car with automatic gears before its driver pushes down the accelerator.

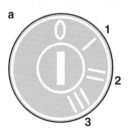

ROUTINE CHECKS

Your driving test examiner will not expect you to
demonstrate that you know how to make the following
checks. The best way to prevent problems occurring,
however, is to maintain your car. Make regular routine
checks and have your car serviced by a qualified
mechanic as recommended by the manufacturers.

Daily checks

- Fuel level. Keep the fuel gauge well above 'empty';
  use only the right type and grade of fuel for your car;
  and fill up before a long drive.
- Brakes.
- Lights and reflectors.
- Mirrors, windows and windscreen.

Periodic checks

These should be checked daily if you drive a great deal,
and during any long car journeys. The illustration
shows the location of each component in a typical car;
check your vehicle handbook if the location differs.

- If the dipstick (**a**) shows that the engine oil level is
  low, unscrew the cap on the engine and top up with
  oil as advised in the vehicle handbook. This also
  advises on lubricant for the gearbox, rear axle and
  power-assisted steering pump reservoir, which should
  usually be checked by a mechanic.
- Unscrew the radiator cap (**b**) and top up if necessary
  with a mixture of water and antifreeze (apart from
  preventing freezing, antifreeze inhibits corrosion). Do not
  unscrew the cap or add cold water if the engine is hot.
- Add brake fluid (**c**) (or have your brakes checked by
  a garage).

- Top up each battery cell (**d**) with distilled water if necessary, just covering the plates. Many batteries are sealed and need no replenishing. Check that the terminals are firm and well greased.
- Top up the bottles of liquid for washing the windscreen and rear window, if necessary (**e**).
- At least weekly, check that tyre pressure (**f**) matches the handbook's specification, and that tyres have the legal minimum depth of tread (1.6 mm) and no deep cuts or other serious defects.
- Filters and spark plugs (**g**) need replacing at intervals laid down in the vehicle handbook.
- Check that your numberplates (**h**) are clean.

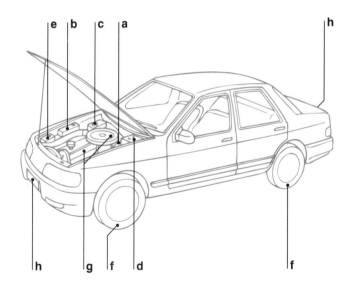

DEFECTS AND THEIR DETECTION

Once you are driving, it will help to be able to identify
important defects. Unless you can easily fix these
yourself, have them repaired by a qualified mechanic.
If worrying sounds or other signs make you think your
vehicle could be unroadworthy, get help before driving
further.

Steering

- 'Wandering', slewing, 'heaviness' or a thumping
  sound could mean an underinflated or punctured tyre.
  After a puncture change the wheel and have the
  faulty tyre repaired or replaced.
- Vibration at certain speeds means that a front wheel
  is unbalanced. Get a garage to fix this.
- Undue play in the steering wheel suggests a fault in
  the mechanism. Get expert help at once.

Tyres

- Uneven wear might indicate misaligned or
  unbalanced wheels, or defective braking, steering or
  suspension.
- Replace defective tyres at once, fitting radial-ply or
  cross-ply to match the other tyres (radial give the best
  grip on wet roads). Never mix both types on one axle.
  If you must use two of each tyre type, put the radials
  on the back. If in doubt, get help from a tyre
  specialist.

Suspension

A vehicle you can bounce up and down excessively
might have worn shock absorbers. Get them checked.

Engine

- If this refuses to start:
  - You might have run out of fuel: check the fuel gauge.
  - You might have flooded the engine by pumping the accelerator too hard. Wait a while and try again.
  - Damp might be affecting the electrical circuits: apply an anti-damp spray.
  - The battery may be flat. The remedy could be a jump start, a push start, or a new battery. If you had left the headlamps on while parked overnight, the battery might recover if you switch off the lights and wait for a while.
- If the starter just clicks, its motor is jammed. You may be able to free it by rocking the car to and fro in second or third gear but with the engine switched off.
- A high engine temperature or vapour rising from under the bonnet may indicate that the engine is overheating. Likely causes are a leaky hose, a broken fan belt, a blown fuse on the fan or a crack in the radiator. Replace a faulty hose or temporarily tape over the break. Replace a broken fan or use a woman's stocking as a temporary replacement. Pour a sealant into a cracked radiator to stop leaking. Replace a blown fuse.
- If the engine seems to be squealing, the cause is a slipping fan belt or alternator belt. Replace it.

Cooling system

If the radiator needs frequent topping up, there may be a fault in the cooling system. Get it checked.

Exhaust system

A loud, throaty engine sound or smoky exhaust fumes
probably means part of the exhaust system is corroded
or broken and needs replacing.

Brakes

- If you have to pull the handbrake up higher than the
  handbook specifies, the cable might need adjusting or
  renewing. Get it checked by a garage.
- If you have to push the brake pedal down farther than
  normal before it starts acting, the brake fluid level is
  low. Get it checked by a garage.
- If the car pulls to one side when you brake, the brakes
  need adjusting.
- If a brake warning light shows, brake fluid might be
  leaking, or a brake pad or shoe might be worn. Get
  the fault checked. If the brakes still work, get the car
  to a garage at once to have the faults mended.

Lights and reflectors

- If a lamp fails to light, check for fuse or bulb failure
  and have the faulty item replaced.
- If a headlamp's main or dipped beam does not work,
  check the unit and fit a replacement.
- If a headlamp's main beam is too low to show the
  road ahead, or so high it dazzles oncoming drivers,
  get it adjusted.
- If an indicator stops working, or flashes irregularly,
  try replacing the bulb. If that doesn't work, or if a
  warning light stays on for no obvious reason, have
  the light and its circuit checked and any faulty item
  replaced.
- Replace broken reflectors.

Horn
If this sounds faintly or not at all, get it fixed.

THE HIGHWAY CODE SAYS:

- You MUST ensure that your vehicle is roadworthy. Take special care of lights, brakes, steering, tyres (including spare), exhaust system, seat belts, demisters, windscreen wipers and washers. Keep windscreens, windows, lights, indicators, reflectors, mirrors and numberplates clean and clear.

EMERGENCY EQUIPMENT

Always carry the following items:
- fire extinguisher
- first-aid kit
- jump leads
- warning triangle
- vinyl tape
- wire
- water-filled plastic container
- tow rope
- spare bulbs and fuses
- pliers
- torch

In winter, in addition to the above, take:
- shovel (for snow)
- sacks (to stop wheels slipping in snow)
- rug and thermos of hot drink
- defrosting and de-icing aids for locks and windows

2. Beginning to drive

LEGAL REQUIREMENTS

The learner driver

The law states that as a learner driver you must comply with the following conditions.

- You must be aged at least 17, or 16 if you receive a mobility allowance. You must hold a valid, signed provisional driving licence for the type of vehicle you will be driving. Most post offices supply application forms for provisional licences.
- You must be accompanied by someone aged at least 21 who has held a full licence for at least three years to drive the type of vehicle you will be driving.
- You must not drive on motorways.

The car you drive

Many people learn to drive in someone else's car. The law states that, whoever owns it, the car you drive must comply with the following conditions:

- It must be legally roadworthy.
- It must have a valid MOT test certificate if old enough to require one.
- It must be licensed correctly.
- It must display a valid tax disc correctly.
- While you are driving, it must display standard-size L-plates (see illustration opposite), one visible from behind and one on the front of the car but not fixed to its windows; this would interfere with your view of the road.

Where to position L-plates

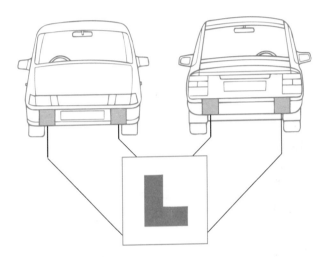

- It must be insured for you as a learner to drive. Check the car's existing insurance policy; it might not cover additional drivers. If necessary, arrange cover with the insurance company already insuring the car, or through an insurance broker. The younger the driver, the more powerful the car, and the more risks insured against, the higher the cost will be. More detailed information on how to arrange insurance is given on p.212. Choose one of the three types of cover. Each insures you against injuring other people and their property, including vehicles.

TAKING INSTRUCTION

Any car driver aged over 21 who has held a full
licence for three years may legally teach you to
drive. Some people learn driving from friends or
relatives. Others find this causes family friction.
Many combine such tuition with paid lessons from an
approved driving instructor (ADI); local inquiries
will probably give you several suitable names.
Be sure to take a planned course of regular lessons
graded to match your increasing experience.

What you should do

- Before taking your first drive, familiarize yourself
  with the controls as described in Chapter 1.
- If possible, learn in a car like the one you expect to
  drive when you have passed the driving test.
- Try to take your first driving practice in a safe space
  such as a grass field or empty car park.
- As you gain confidence, move on to increasingly
  busy roads of all types – except motorways – to gain
  traffic experience as described in the following
  chapters.
- Practise as often as possible.

What your instructor should do

- Your instructor will get you to pull in to the side
  somewhere safe before discussing any fresh kind of
  problem to be tackled.
- The instructor should do the same if your reaction to
  a particular situation was wrong. After explaining
  what should have been done, the instructor should
  ask you to repeat the explanation to prove you have
  learned the lesson.

STARTING THE ENGINE

Begin learning to drive in an open space where you
can safely practise starting, stopping and steering.

- Before starting the engine, check that the handbrake
  is on and the gear lever is in neutral.

Starting a cold engine

- If the engine is cold and your car has a manual choke
  control, pull this out before turning the ignition key.
- Turn the key clockwise all the way until the engine
  fires. Take your hand off the ignition key at once.
- When the engine is running well, push the choke
  control (if you have one) in steadily before the engine
  starts making a heavy chugging sound. Leaving the
  choke out too long would flood the engine with fuel,
  making it stall (or 'cut out').
- To keep a cold engine running, you might need to
  press the accelerator pedal a little. If you overdo it
  this will also flood the engine and cause it to stall.
- If the engine does not start first time, turn off the
  ignition and check that all nonessential electrical
  items are switched off. Then wait a few seconds and
  turn the ignition key again for up to five seconds.
  Repeat several times if necessary. Pressing down the
  clutch pedal as you turn the key might help.
- If a cold engine refuses to start, see p.35 for possible
  causes and their remedies.

Starting a warm engine

- To start an engine that has already warmed up, turn
  the ignition key as before. You will not need to use a
  manual choke if you have one, but you might need to
  press down on the accelerator slightly.

PREPARING TO GO

When its engine is running your car will not move until you have put it in gear and released the handbrake.

- Make sure all doors are shut, seat and mirrors are adjusted, and seat belts are on.
- Put both hands on the steering wheel (**a**).
- Press down the clutch pedal with your left foot to disconnect the engine from the gearbox (**b**).
- Keep your foot pressing down on the clutch pedal.
- With your left hand put the gear lever into first gear. (In most cars this means pushing the lever far left then up. In other cars this is the position for reverse gear; middle and up is the position for first gear. The gear lever should be clearly labelled with a diagram showing the position of each gear.)
- Because you are still pressing down the clutch pedal, the engine is still disconnected from the gearbox.
- Place your left hand back on the steering wheel.

a

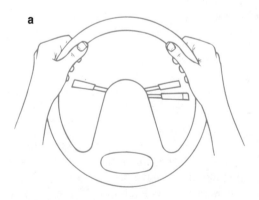

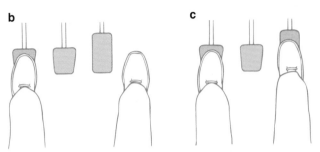

- Gently press the accelerator pedal with your right foot (**c**) until you hear the engine sound change as the revolutions per minute increase. Pressing the pedal down a quarter of the way should be enough.
- You are now looking ahead, with both hands on the steering wheel. The handbrake is still on.
- Using your left heel as a pivot, let the clutch pedal rise smoothly until a slight drop in engine pitch tells you that you have reached the biting point, where the disengaged clutch plate begins to mesh with the plate that is already turning, and itself starts to revolve.
- Keep the clutch pedal at the biting point and the accelerator pedal partly pressed down.

SETTING OFF FOR THE FIRST TIME

You have now reached the point where you are ready to move off with your car fully under control. Before setting off, always make the following safety checks, with the handbrake on and the gear lever in first.

- Check that the road ahead is clear.
- Switch on your indicator.
- Check the road behind in your mirrors, and also look

back over your right shoulder to make sure all is clear behind.

- Look forward again to check that the road ahead is clear.

Immediately after completing the safety checks, use the following procedure to set off:

- Grasp the handbrake with your left hand and smoothly release it.
- Place your left hand back on the steering wheel.
- Keep the clutch and accelerator pedals partly pressed down as already described. The car should not start to move yet.
- If the car starts moving forward, press the clutch pedal a bit more but keep the accelerator still partly pressed down. If the engine pitch drops below biting-point level, reset the handbrake, fully press down the clutch pedal, put the gear lever back in neutral, and take your feet off the clutch and accelerator pedals. Then go through the starting sequence again, including the safety checks.
- Next, let the clutch pedal rise slightly until the engine

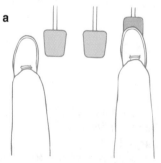

a

is transmitting just enough force to the car's wheels to make it creep forward.

- To increase speed, release the clutch pedal all the way. Do it smoothly, not jerkily, or the car will leap, perhaps making the engine stall.
- Press smoothly on the accelerator to bring the car up to its maximum speed in first gear (about 7–10 mph).
- Take your left foot off the clutch pedal and place it on the floor to the left of the pedal (**a**) or between your seat and the pedal. (Leaving your foot on the pedal would cause undue wear on a bearing.)

SLOW-SPEED DRIVING

Practise clutch and accelerator control by driving in first gear at very slow speeds. Complete clutch control is the key to coping with junctions and driving in traffic. At low speed, precise control of the accelerator helps to prevent the car bounding along like a kangaroo.

Clutch control

- Set off as already described and drive along in first gear at a walking pace.
- Keep the accelerator pedal pressed down a little.
- Vary your speed by easing the clutch pedal very slightly up and down.
- Practise this until you can keep the car barely creeping forward.

Accelerator control

- Set off in first gear, with the clutch pedal fully released.
- Gently decrease acceleration until your car barely creeps forward.

- Then gently press down on the accelerator pedal to gain speed. If you keep your right foot's heel on the floor to act as a pivot, you should achieve precise accelerator control.
- Later, you can apply the same methods of accelerator control in second and reverse gears.

SLOWING DOWN AND STOPPING

Travel slowly in first gear with your right foot lightly pressing down on the accelerator pedal. Drive three or four car lengths, then make your first stop.

- Lift your right foot off the accelerator.
- With your right foot gently press the foot brake (**a**).

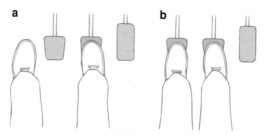

- At the same time, fully press down on the clutch pedal with your left foot and keep it held down (**b**).
- When the car stops, apply the handbrake. You can then remove your right foot from the brake pedal.
- Put the gear lever in neutral.
- Release the clutch pedal.
- To switch off the engine, turn the ignition key anticlockwise until you can pull it out.
- Start again, drive slowly, and stop again.
- Repeat until the actions become automatic.

STEERING

As you drive, hold the steering wheel firmly but lightly with both hands in the 'ten-to-two' or 'quarter-to-three' position. Look well ahead to judge when and how much to turn. Use the following procedures to turn left and right. Don't remove your hands from the wheel, and don't cross hands.

To turn left

- Slide your left hand up the left side of the steering wheel toward the top but no farther (**a**).
- With your left hand, pull the wheel down and to the left (**b**).
- Meanwhile, slide your right hand down the right side of the wheel (**c**).
- With your right hand, push the wheel up (**d**). Meanwhile, slide your left hand up the wheel again (**e**).
- For a sharp left-hand turn repeat this sequence.

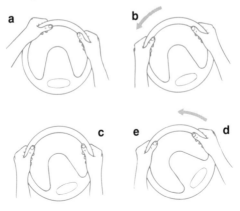

To turn right

- Slide your right hand up the right side of the wheel toward the top but no farther (**a**).
- With your right hand, pull the wheel down and to the right (**b**).
- Meanwhile, slide your left hand down the left side of the wheel (**c**).
- With your left hand, push the wheel up (**d**). Meanwhile slide your right hand up the wheel again (**e**).
- For a sharp right-hand turn repeat this sequence.

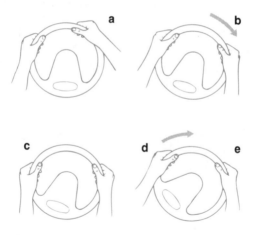

After turning

Straighten up by turning the steering wheel back again, using hand movements opposite those used for turning. The wheel may tend to spin back on its own, but hold it firmly to stay in control.

CHANGING GEARS

To increase speed, you will need to change up through
the gears. Different gears work best at different speeds
but their ranges overlap. Below we give typical speeds
for using four forward gears. Drivers use a gear's
highest speed only to gain extra acceleration, as when
overtaking. A fifth gear, if available, saves fuel when
you cruise at 40 mph and above.

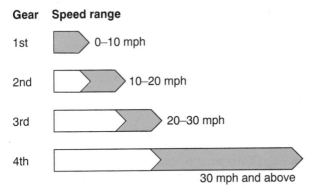

Gear	Speed range
1st	0–10 mph
2nd	10–20 mph
3rd	20–30 mph
4th	30 mph and above

Changing up

You can practise engaging gears 2–4 without reaching
more than about 20 mph. To do this and stop you need
a clear space about 250 m (273 yd) long. To change
down before stopping you need a considerably longer
distance.

- With the engine switched off and the clutch pedal
  pressed down, practise grasping the gear lever
  without looking at it, and change up and down
  through the gears to learn their positions.
- Return the gear lever to neutral.

- Start the engine and set off in first gear.
- Accelerate to about 5 mph.
- Press down the clutch pedal beyond the biting point. You need not press it all the way down. At the same time, lift your foot off the accelerator pedal.
- Without looking down, grasp the gear lever and change up firmly from first to second gear.
- Let the clutch pedal up smoothly but slowly. At the same time, press the accelerator pedal to maintain momentum.
- Accelerate to about 10 mph.
- Repeat the previous four steps, but this time engage third gear and accelerate to about 15 mph.
- Repeat once more, but this time engage fourth gear and accelerate to 20 mph.

Changing down

Practise changing down through the gears as you slow down but not while going too fast for the gears you are engaging. Downchanging has a braking effect, but it also makes you ready to speed up again if you wish. Drivers often change down a gear and accelerate to put on a burst of speed for overtaking.

- To change down from fourth to third gear, brake down to the correct speed for the gear, then press the clutch. At the same time, let the accelerator pedal rise.
- Grasp the gear lever without looking down, and change down firmly from fourth to third gear.
- Let the clutch up smoothly but slowly. Don't speed up.
- When you have slowed down enough, repeat the previous three steps but this time engage second gear.
- When you have slowed down to walking pace, repeat once more but this time engage first gear.

REVERSING

Begin practising reversing in an empty car park, a field,
or another open space where you can learn to drive
backward without fear of hitting a kerb or a road user if
you make a mistake. If no such space is available,
practise in a quiet road free of parked cars and with a
low kerb. A broad cul-de-sac might be suitable.
Wherever you start, choose a level surface.

Before you start

If practising in an open space, try to mark off a stretch
about 70 m (77 yd) long and 7 m (about 8 yd) wide as
an imitation road. Its 'kerbs' could be two lengths of
thick rope or broad tape laid parallel to each other and
weighed down with stones.

General rules for reversing

- Keep looking backward, but glance briefly all around
  as you go.
- Keep your speed down to walking pace.
- Never reverse farther than necessary.
- Always give way to other road users.

Reversing straight back

- Stop about 1 m (about 1 yd) from the left-hand kerb.
- Check that the road is clear of other vehicles and
  there are no pedestrians behind you – especially
  children. Switch off the engine and get out of the car
  to look, if necessary.
- With the handbrake still on, and the clutch pedal fully
  pressed down, put the car into reverse gear.
- Shift your body slightly to the left in your seat, if
  necessary removing your seat belt.
- Look all around again as a safety check.

- Look back through the rear window over your left shoulder to watch where you are going.
- Smoothly release the handbrake as you let the clutch pedal up just enough for the car to crawl backward at the speed of a slow walk.
- With your right hand near the top of the steering wheel and your left hand low down on the left, try to steer a straight course 1 m (about 1 yd) out from the kerb (**a**). Because steering still turns the front wheels, turning the steering wheel will now make the new 'rear' (the true front) of the car (**b**) swing out more than its 'front' (the true rear). At first you will tend to wander from side to side.

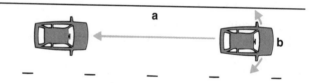

- Straighten up by making very slight steering corrections.
- Keep practising until you can reverse at a slow walking speed parallel and close to the kerb for 50 m (about 55 yd) or more.
- Repeat at a moderate walking pace, with your foot off the clutch pedal, but be prepared to press the brake pedal if necessary to slow down if your course falters.

PARKING PRACTICE

Parking beside an artificial kerb

In a safe, open space, practise stopping with your car parallel to a rope or tape 'kerb', and about two tyre widths out.

- Attempt this exercise first while driving slowly forward.
- Then repeat, driving slowly backward.
- Each time you stop, get out to check how near you are to the tape or rope, and whether your car is parallel to it.
- When you have mastered this manoeuvre, try to park only one tyre width out from your 'kerb'.

Entering a garage or gateway

In a safe, open space, practise driving in and out of an artificial gateway or garage entrance made of two stacks of cardboard boxes separated by a gap 50 cm (20 in) wider than your car. This exercise helps to give you a good sense of the width of your car.

- Approach your 'gateway' head on and drive through it at a slow walking pace (**a**).

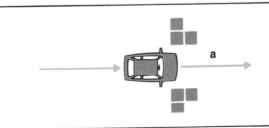

- Reverse through the 'gateway' at a safe speed.
- Repeat these exercises until you can carry them out at normal walking speed.
- Starting with the car approaching as if from a road running perpendicular to your 'gateway', make a forward turn to pass through it.
- Repeat this manoeuvre, but in reverse.
- Starting ever closer to the 'gateway', see how sharply you can turn to pass through without touching the 'gateway's' sides. You will need to drive very slowly and turn the steering wheel hard.
- If necessary, stop and get out to assess the situation. Rather than risk scraping your car on the 'gateway' (which would cause damage if it were a real entrance), go backward (or forward, if reversing into the entrance) and try to pass through it again.

Parking in car parks

In a safe, open space, practise parking in an area with three sides representing the wall and adjacent cars in a space in a car park.

- First, drive forward to stop just in front of a 'wall' made of cardboard boxes (**a**). Try to leave a gap of a

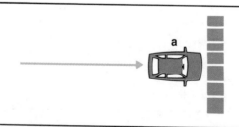

hand's width between the wall and your car.

- Repeat this exercise in reverse. This practice helps to give you a sense of the length of your car.
- Make an artificial car parking space, marked out on the ground with boxes, tapes or ropes. Driving slowly, practise parking inside this without crossing its sides or closed end (**b**). This practice helps to give you a sense of both the length and the width of your car.

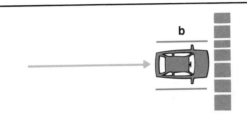

Other manoeuvres

You could also arrange boxes and tapes to practise other open space manoeuvres before trying these out on a road. (For turning and parking on roads, see pp.88–99 and pp.117–23.)

- Practise reverse parking behind an imitation car made of boxes to park alongside a rope or tape 'kerb'.
- Practise reversing into a space by an artificial kerb between two imitation cars.
- Practise reversing from an artificial road left into an artificial side road, then driving forward and turning right.
- Practise making a three-point turn in an artificial road, without touching its kerbs.

3. On the road

LEARNING STRATEGY

The following guidelines offer a basic approach to learning to drive on the road.

- Before taking to the road, read this book and study the Highway Code to familiarize yourself with the conditions you will encounter and the best ways to cope with them. Breaching the Highway Code can be grounds for a traffic offence, even though the code itself is not law.
- While being driven by qualified drivers (friends or relatives or professional instructors) get them to describe what they are doing and why, as they negotiate different road situations. Notice how they plan ahead when they signal, brake, change gear and position the car for a turn.
- If being taught by friends or relatives they must be over age 21 and with three years' experience.
- Drive whenever you get the chance.
- Drive no more than an hour or so a day at first to avoid tiredness and loss of concentration.
- When you drive keep checking the traffic and road conditions ahead and behind.
- Use what you see ahead to help you predict when you will need to move out, speed up, slow down or stop.
- Before making any of these manoeuvres check your mirrors and make the appropriate signal.
- Make your manoeuvre only if it is safe to do so.
- Watch the road all the time, but pay heed to your teacher's instructions.

- Start on quiet roads but later get practice on both rural and urban roads if possible, including dual carriageways (but not motorways).
- Before taking your test, try to clock up thousands of miles of hands-on experience.

GIVING SIGNALS

Signalling alerts other road users to your intentions when you wish to change course or speed. Drivers mostly signal using direction indicators and brake lights. Headlights, horn and arm signals (see pp.58–9) can also be used.

Using indicators and brake lights

- Use a direction indicator well ahead of your manoeuvre, especially if you wish to overtake, shift lanes or turn left or right.
- Pressing the foot brake automatically switches on brake lights, warning the traffic behind that you are slowing or stopping.

Using headlights

- Switch headlights quickly on and off to show other road users you are there in tricky situations where others might not notice your car or hear your horn or where sounding the horn is illegal.

Using the horn

- Sound the horn to warn others you are there only when essential, as before bends on a narrow lane or if a vehicle is backing into you while you are stopped.

Emergency vehicles' signals

Be alert for the warning sirens and flashing blue lights of emergency vehicles. If you see or hear one approaching, pull in to let it past.

USING ARM SIGNALS

Here we show arm signals used by drivers and traffic controllers.

Arm signals warning other road users

Drivers use recognized arm signals less than they used to. These sometimes still serve a purpose, however, by reinforcing direction indicators or brake lights.

- Right arm extended horizontally to the right (**a**): 'I intend moving to the right or turning right'. Use this when about to turn right after overtaking a stationary vehicle or when about to turn right on a road where traffic is moving at speed.
- Right arm extended right and rotated anticlockwise (**b**): 'I intend moving left or turning left'.

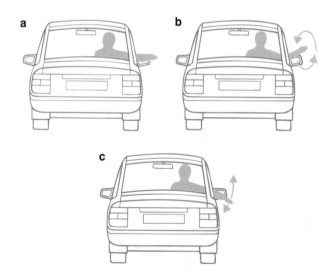

● Right arm extended and moved up and down (**c**): 'I intend slowing down or stopping'. Use this to warn drivers and waiting pedestrians before you slow down or stop at a zebra crossing or stop after using your left-turn indicator.

Drivers' arm signals to traffic controllers
Drivers use these to indicate their intention to police or other persons who are controlling traffic.
● Left arm raised vertically from the elbow, palm forward (**d**): 'I intend driving straight on'.
● Left arm extended horizontally to the left (**e**): 'I intend turning left'.
● Right arm extended horizontally to the right (**f**): 'I intend turning right'.

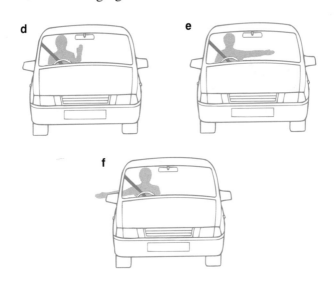

Traffic controllers' signals to road users

Police or other authorized traffic controllers use arm signals to stop traffic or to beckon it on.

- To stop traffic approaching from behind (**a**).
- To stop traffic approaching from the front (**b**).
- To stop traffic approaching from the front and behind (**c**).
- To beckon on traffic approaching from the front (**d**).
- To beckon on traffic approaching from the side (**e**).
- To beckon on traffic approaching from behind (**f**).

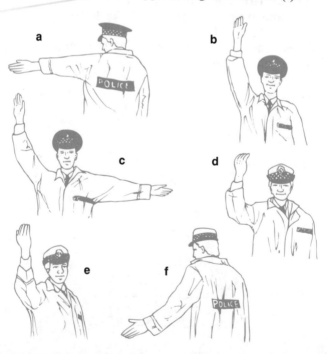

SIGNALLING *DOS* AND *DON'TS*

- Do use only the signals described.
- Do signal to tell other road users your intentions to change direction, slow or stop.
- Do signal early enough to give others time to react safely.
- Do signal long enough for people to notice.
- Do cancel your signal when it is no longer needed.
- Do not signal too soon. A following driver might expect you to turn off earlier than you intend.
- Do not signal so late that following vehicles must swerve or brake hard to avoid you.
- Do not signal if there is no one to see you or if a signal would perplex other road users.
- Do not signal to overtake parked vehicles if you are positioned to steer straight past them.
- Do not wave pedestrians across a road.
- Do not flash headlights to scare or instruct.
- Do not assume another driver's flashed headlights invite you to go ahead. The driver might have flashed them by mistake or at another driver.
- Do not sound your horn aggressively, between 11.30 pm and 7.00 am in built-up areas, or when stopped unless a moving vehicle could hit yours.

TRAFFIC SIGNS

Different types of traffic signs order, warn or inform. Besides traffic signs and lights on posts there are distinctive road markings which indicate such things as no overtaking or no waiting. You must gain a sound knowledge of what all traffic signs mean. Here we explain shapes and colours of the main classes of traffic sign displayed on posts. For full-colour guides to all traffic signs see the HMSO publications *Know Your Traffic Signs* and *The Highway Code*.

Classes of traffic sign

Each shape means a different thing:

- **Circular** signs (**a**) give orders – e.g. concerning speed limits, parking restrictions, no entry, no right (or left or U) turn and no stopping.
- **Triangular** signs (**b**) warn of such things as stop or give-way lines, roundabouts, bends and steep hills ahead.
- **Rectangular** signs (**c**) inform; most give directions.

In addition, each colour means a different thing:

- Signs with **red** circles or rings forbid.
- Signs with **blue** circles give positive instructions.
- Signs with **blue** rectangles give general information.
- Signs with **green** rectangles on primary routes give directional information.

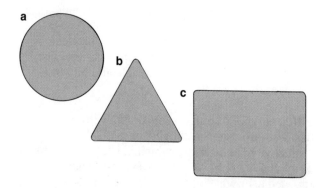

MOVING OFF

- Before driving off from a kerb, make sure doors are shut, seat, seat belts, and mirrors are adjusted, handbrake is on, and gear lever is in neutral.
- Check that the road ahead is clear (**a**).
- Switch on your offside ('right turn') indicator (**b**).
- Check the road behind in your mirrors (**c**).
- If all seems clear, put the car into first gear, but keep your foot on the clutch and keep the handbrake on.
- Look back over your right shoulder to make sure all is still clear behind.
- Look forward again to check the road ahead.

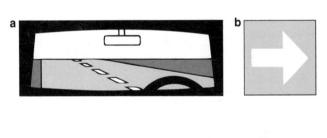

- If a vehicle or pedestrian appears during your visual checks, making you wait for a while, change back into neutral gear, take your foot off the clutch pedal, and stop signalling. Then signal, re-engage first gear, and repeat your visual checks.
- If all is clear, release the handbrake and move off slowly, leaving the kerb at a slight angle (**d**).
- Smoothly accelerate on the left-hand side of the road. Switch off your indicator.
- Practise moving off from behind a parked car. You will have to pull out quite sharply, so be prepared to wait for oncoming traffic. And be careful not to hit the parked car's offside rear corner.

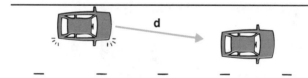

THE HIGHWAY CODE SAYS:

- Use your mirrors before you move off.
- Signal if necessary before moving out.
- Look round as well for a final check.
- Only move off when it is safe to do so.

STARTING ON HILLS

On hill starts allow for the effects of gravity. Practise uphill and downhill starts on a gentle slope in a quiet road.

Starting uphill

- On uphill starts press the accelerator harder than you would on a level road before raising the clutch pedal to its biting point, with the gear lever in first gear.
- As the engine pitch drops, press the accelerator pedal a bit harder still.
- The car should now remain stationary in first gear when you release the handbrake.
- If the car rolls back downhill, quickly press the foot brake and clutch and apply the handbrake.
- When you have mastered keeping the car stationary in first gear with the handbrake off you are ready to drive off, but wait for a large traffic gap as you will gain speed more slowly than on a level road.

Starting downhill

- On downhill starts, you should not need to use the accelerator pedal at first.
- Press the clutch pedal.
- Select second gear.
- Press the foot brake pedal.
- Release the handbrake and, when it is safe to move off, the foot brake and the clutch.
- On a shallow slope, accelerate gently away.
- On a steep slope, do not accelerate, but let your second gear act as a brake to slow your descent.
- On a very steep slope use the foot brake to keep your speed down.

POSITIONING ON THE ROAD

Position in road

- You must normally drive on the left.
- On a dual carriageway you must normally drive in the middle of the left-hand lane (overtaking is explained on pp.76–80).

Position in lane

- On a two-way, single carriageway, stay at least half a metre ($1^1/_2$–2 ft) out from the side (**a**).
- Avoid driving very close to the edge (**b**): your car might hit the kerb or pedestrians. Also, broken glass or a nail might puncture a tyre.
- Avoid driving close to the middle of the road (**c**). Your car obstructs overtaking vehicles and you risk hitting oncoming traffic.
- On wide main roads drive a bit more toward the middle of the road than on narrower roads, especially in towns or at high speed in the country. This position improves visibility, increasing reaction time and reducing the risk of hitting pedestrians who stray off the kerb.

Parked vehicles and other obstructions

- On a two-way single carriageway stop behind obstructions such as parked vehicles to let oncoming vehicles pass, but leave enough room in front to pull away. First check your mirror, and signal if necessary, to alert drivers behind you that you intend to stop. Pull in no more than you have to so that you do not have to pull out at an abrupt angle. Try to stop well before the parked vehicle to widen your view of the road ahead.

a

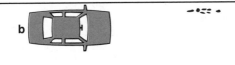

b

c

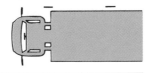

- Unless obstructed by oncoming traffic, steer a straight course as you drive past a row of parked vehicles: do not weave in and out.
- When passing parked vehicles, drive slowly on narrow roads, and leave enough space in case pedestrians run out between the vehicles, or one vehicle starts moving, or its door opens.

THE HIGHWAY CODE SAYS:

- Keep to the left, except where road signs or markings indicate otherwise or when you want to overtake, turn right or pass parked vehicles or pedestrians in the road. Let others overtake if they want to.
- You must not drive on a pavement or footpath except for access to property.

DRIVING ALONG

While driving along a main road observe the following guidelines:

- Observe maximum speed limits (see table opposite).
- Keep up with the flow of traffic, but be aware of the speed limit and don't try to keep up with cars going over the limit.
- Do not drive so slowly that a long queue of vehicles builds up behind you.
- Drive within the safe stopping limits.
- Know what's going on at the back as well as at the front. Frequently glance in your mirrors to check following vehicles and before you slow down, speed up, or manoeuvre.

Maximum speed limits (mph)

Vehicle type	Built-up area	Single carriageway	Dual carriageway	Motorway
Cars	30	60	70	70
Cars towing caravans or trailers	30	50	60	60
Buses and coaches	30	50	60	70
Light goods vehicles	30	50	60	70
Heavy goods vehicles	30	40	50	60

- Watch out for cycles and motorcycles, and allow them plenty of room.
- Watch out for vehicles or pedestrians emerging from side roads or drives (**a**).

THE HIGHWAY CODE SAYS:

- Drive at a speed that will allow you to stop well within the distance you can see to be clear.
- You MUST NOT exceed the maximum speed limits for the road and for your vehicle. The presence of street lights usually indicates a 30 mph speed limit unless signs show other limits.
- Drive slowly in residential areas. In some roads there are features such as road humps and narrowings to slow you down. A 20 mph maximum speed limit may also be in force.
- A speed limit does not mean it is safe to drive at that speed. Drive according to the conditions. Slow down if the road is wet or icy or if it is foggy. Drive more slowly at night when it is harder to see pedestrians and cyclists.

DRIVING AROUND BENDS

Approaching a bend

Watch well ahead for road signs or road markings –
such as the word SLOW – which might indicate bends.
Notice if a sign indicates:

- A bend to the left (**a**).
- A bend to the right (**b**).
- A series of bends (**c**).
- A sharp deviation of route (**d**).

Expect dangers ahead, including:

- Adverse camber (the road slopes down toward a
  bend's outside edge).
- Slow vehicles obscured by a bend.
- Vehicles stopped or parked on a bend.
- Pedestrians walking on the road.

Also, it is important to know how your car handles a
bend. Various factors – including tyre pressure and
load – can affect steering.

Preparing for the bend

- Check your mirror to see how close any vehicles are behind you.
- Approach a left-hand bend in the middle of your traffic lane (**e**).
- Approach a right-hand bend keeping toward the left side of your traffic lane (**f**).
- Reduce speed by decelerating, with a touch on the foot brake so brake lights warn drivers behind.
- If necessary, slow down by steadily applying the foot brake and changing into a lower gear.
- Reach your lowest speed at the start of the bend.

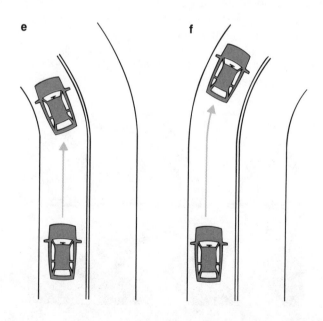

- Approach the bend slowly enough to make an orderly stop if you meet an obstruction.

Driving around a bend
- At the start of the bend press the accelerator pedal no more than enough to keep the car moving along at a safe speed.
- Look out for dangers. Be aware that you can see into a right-hand bend, but left-hand bends are blind.
- Avoid (destabilizing) braking while rounding a bend, except in an emergency.

Stopping on bends
- Never normally stop on a bend.
- If you must stop on a bend, stop where following vehicles will see you.
- If you must park on a bend, keep off the unbroken centre line if there is one. Switch on hazard warning lights and, if possible, display a red warning triangle to alert oncoming vehicles.

DRIVING UPHILL AND DOWNHILL
- The force of gravity affects vehicle speeds on hills.
- Uphill, gravity tends to slow you down. To compensate you will need to accelerate harder or change down, or both.
- Downhill, gravity makes you accelerate. You might need to decelerate and change down or brake, or both.

Driving uphill
Tackle a hill climb in this way:
- Before you reach it, assess a hill's likely effects on your speed.

- Especially watch out for signs warning of a long hill, bends on a hill, or a steep hill, with the gradient shown as a percentage (**a**) or ratio (**b**). A sign showing 10% (1:10) means a vertical rise of one foot for every ten feet you drive.

a

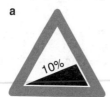

b

- Look out for slow vehicles ahead.
- Change down, if necessary, to maintain climbing power. On a steep or twisting hill you might need to change down more than once (**c**). Make changes quickly to avoid losing momentum between gears.
- Drive at a safe distance behind the vehicle ahead in case it stops or slows down without warning.
- Overtake only if you can accelerate rapidly and safely past the vehicle ahead; on dual carriageways avoid slow overtaking that holds up vehicles behind.
- If you must slow down or stop remember that braking or decelerating uphill slows you down faster than it would on a flat surface.
- If you stop, avoid moving backwards by engaging the handbrake before disengaging the foot brake.

Driving downhill
Tackle a hill descent in this way:
- Watch out for signs warning of steep hills and suggesting engaging low gears.

- Change down, if necessary, at the top of a hill. The steeper the hill, the lower the gear you should use (**d**). Changing down reduces the need to brake hard, which can cause wear, making brakes ineffective.
- Drive at a safe distance behind the vehicle ahead. Remember that slowing down is harder downhill than it is on a flat surface.
- Overtake only if this is safe, and drop back if the vehicle ahead speeds up.

Appropriate gear for the hill gradient

Uphill

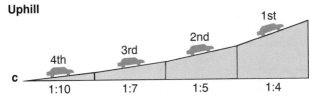

| 1:10 | 1:7 | 1:5 | 1:4 |

Downhill

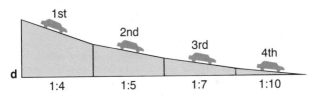

| 1:4 | 1:5 | 1:7 | 1:10 |

THE HIGHWAY CODE SAYS:

- On some hills an extra uphill 'crawler' lane may be provided to prevent slower vehicles holding up traffic. Use this lane if you are driving a slow-moving vehicle or if there are vehicles behind you wishing to overtake.

OVERTAKING

Overtake only when necessary, on a safe stretch of
road, and if you are sure you can overtake quickly.
Careless overtaking could mean hitting an oncoming
vehicle – a major cause of serious accidents. (For
passing parked vehicles see 'Positioning on the road',
pp.66–8.)

- Normally you should overtake on the right.
- You may overtake on the left only:
  - When the vehicle ahead signals a right turn and it is
    safe for you to pass on its left (unless the left-hand
    lane is a bus lane and you would be forced into it
    during its hours of use).
  - When you are in a lane of slow-moving traffic
    moving faster than the lane to its right.
  - When you move into an inside lane to turn left and
    traffic to your right is slowing or stopping.
  - When you are in a two-lane one-way street.

Never overtake:

- Where there are double white lines along the middle
  of the road, with an unbroken line nearest to you.
- As you approach a pedestrian, school or rail crossing,
  especially in the zig-zag area at a pedestrian crossing.
- As you approach a junction or roundabout.
- After a NO OVERTAKING sign. In such cases, you
  can overtake only after you pass a sign indicating that
  it is safe to do so.
- Where an obstruction – such as a bend, hill or hump
  bridge – prevents you from seeing if the road ahead is
  clear.
- Where you see 'get left' (or 'keep left') arrows.

Before overtaking

- Keep far enough behind the vehicle ahead to see beyond it.
- Assess the vehicle's length and speed.
- Using mirrors and glancing over your right shoulder, check that nothing is about to overtake you.
- Changing down a gear will boost your acceleration, reducing time spent on the wrong side of the road:
  - Below 20 mph use second gear.
  - Between 20 mph and 45–50 mph use third gear.
  - Above 45–50 mph use fourth gear.
- On a narrow road, you might give a warning hoot first to alert the vehicle ahead of you.
- Edge out for a full view of the road ahead (**a**).

Pull back in if:

- Something is coming in the opposite direction (**b**).
- You lack enough acceleration to pass the vehicle ahead quickly.

- The vehicle ahead turns right or speeds up.
- You are being overtaken.
- You are following a line of vehicles.

- You would make another vehicle slow down or swerve.
- You reach a hidden dip in the road that might hide an oncoming vehicle.
- You see roadworks ahead that interfere with normal traffic flow.
- The road narrows.
- You would drive over chevrons or diagonal stripes marked on the road.
- You encounter any other danger.

While overtaking

- If all is clear, signal with your right indicator (**a**), glance back again, and accelerate smoothly out and past the vehicle ahead (**b**).
- Normally leave more than a door's width between your vehicle and the one you are passing.
- If an oncoming vehicle appears when you have pulled out, decide whether to accelerate hard and press on or indicate left and drop back. Do not hesitate. If in doubt, drop back.

After overtaking

- As soon as you are safely past the vehicle you are overtaking, pull back in (**c**).
- Change back up to the gear you were in before overtaking. Do not slow down.

Overtaking on hills

- Allow extra time for overtaking uphill.
- Be sure you can pull in well before the top of the hill.
- Remember that oncoming traffic could be coming downhill toward you extremely fast.

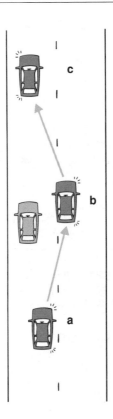

- After you overtake downhill your speed could be
  abnormally high; slow down sooner than normal.
- Take special care overtaking on three-lane roads. On
  long hills some roads have double white lines. Do not
  overtake if the line on your side is unbroken.

THE HIGHWAY CODE SAYS:

- Do not overtake unless you can do so safely. Make sure the road is sufficiently clear both ahead and behind.
- Do not get too close to the vehicle you intend to overtake – it will obscure your view of the road ahead.
- Use your mirrors. Signal before you start to move out.
- Take extra care at night and in poor visibility when it is harder to judge speed and distance.
- Once you have started to overtake, quickly move past the vehicle you are overtaking, leaving it plenty of room. Then move back to the left as soon as you can but do not cut in.
- When overtaking motorcyclists, bicyclists or horse riders, give them at least as much room as you would give a car.
- If in doubt do not overtake.
- Do not increase your speed when you are being overtaken. Slow down if necessary to let the overtaking vehicle pass and pull in.

COPING WITH CROSSINGS

Drivers must give way to pedestrians and trains at their crossings, and must give way to trams.

Pedestrian crossings

These include zebra, pelican, puffin and controlled crossings.

- **Zebra** crossings (**a**) have a flashing yellow beacon on each side of the road, a band of black-and-white stripes across the road surface, and warning zig-zag approach lines ending in a broken give-way line. Drivers must stop at the give-way line when the crossing is being used. Before stopping, the leading driver or motorcyclist should give a slowing-down arm signal.

- **Pelican** crossings (**b**) have pedestrian-controlled traffic lights that go from red to flashing amber to green. Even if a traffic island splits a crossing in half, all counts as one if the crossing is straight. Drivers must stop on a red light and give way to pedestrians crossing while the amber light flashes. If there are no pedestrians, drivers may proceed, cautiously, when the amber light flashes.
- **Puffin** crossings are pedestrian-controlled crossings with lights that go green automatically once a

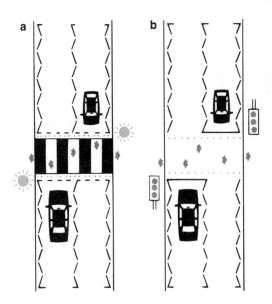

pedestrian has crossed. Puffin crossings have no flashing amber lights.

- Crossings controlled by traffic signals, police or traffic wardens should be driven across only when pedestrians are no longer crossing, even if drivers have had the signal to go ahead.
- Two flashing amber lights warn of some dangerous crossing points – e.g. school patrol.
- At a school patrol, give way to all pedestrians crossing.
- In traffic jams, do not stop your vehicle on a pedestrian crossing.

THE HIGHWAY CODE SAYS:

- As you approach a zebra crossing, look out for people waiting to cross (especially children, elderly people or people with disabilities). Be ready to slow down or stop to let them across.
- When someone has stepped on to a crossing, you MUST give way.
- Allow more time for stopping on wet or icy roads.
- Do not wave people across; this could be dangerous if another vehicle is approaching.
- You must not overtake or park on a zebra or pelican crossing, including the area marked by zig-zag lines.

Train crossings

Level crossings are where railway lines cross a road.

- Most railway level crossings display a steady amber light and two red lights (a) that flash and an alarm that sounds as a train arrives. Some crossings stay open but most have full or half barriers that close the road when a train passes. Never drive in and out of lowered barriers – wait until the red lights stop flashing or the alarm stops sounding and the barriers lift.

- Some crossings have gates but no signals. You must stop when these gates start to shut.
- Some unattended crossings with barriers or gates have STOP signs and small lights. If a red light shows, wait. When a green light shows, open both gates or barriers. Drive across quickly if the green light still shows. Then close the gates or barriers.
- Some unattended crossings have gates but no lights. If you cannot see or hear a train coming use the

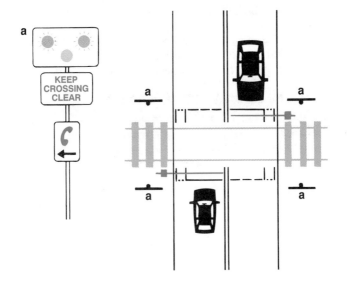

railway telephone to ask the signal operator if you may cross. If it is safe, open both gates, check again for trains, drive across quickly, and close the gates. Tell the signal operator you have crossed.

- At open crossings with only a GIVE WAY sign, look and listen for trains before crossing.
- If your vehicle breaks down or has an accident on the crossing, get everyone out and off the crossing. Ring the signal operator by railway telephone if there is one. Push your car off the crossing if you can but get off it if you see the amber light or hear the alarm.

Tram crossings

- Do not park in the path of trams.
- Keep out of tram lanes.
- If tram stops have platforms, obey road signs and markings.
- If tram stops lack platforms, do not drive between a tram and the kerb to its left.
- Beware pedestrians running out to catch a tram.

THE HIGHWAY CODE SAYS:

- Approach and cross level crossings with care.
- Never drive on to a crossing until the road is clear on the other side – don't drive 'nose to tail' over it.
- Never stop on or just after a crossing. Never park close to a crossing.
- Take extra care when tramways cross from one side of the road to the other and where the road narrows and the tracks come close to the kerb.
- Always give way to trams.

STOPPING DISTANCES

Drive at a speed which allows you to stop safely before any obstruction, for instance a pedestrian crossing the road or a vehicle ahead.

The table on the following page shows the shortest stopping distances in the best conditions – that is, for alert drivers, in cars with good brakes and tyres, driven on dry roads.

- Remember that the faster you drive, the greater the stopping distance you need. At 40 mph brakes take four times the distance needed for stopping at half that speed.

- Stopping distance is made up of two components: thinking distance (the time you take to react and start braking) and braking distance. Even fit people need more than half a second to react.

- Stopping distances are greatly increased if drivers are tired, cars have worn tyres or brakes, or roads are wet, greasy or icy.

- Stopping distances are always longer for motorcycles and lorries than cars.

- If you are alert and are driving a well-maintained car in fast traffic on dry roads, obey the two-second rule: allow a two-second gap between your car and the vehicle in front. At least double this distance on wet roads and increase it still more on icy roads. Estimate the time gap by starting to say 'Only a fool breaks the two-second rule' the moment the vehicle in front passes a fixed point such as a lamppost or road sign. If you reach the same fixed point before finishing the sentence, you are too close to the vehicle.

Table of shortest overall stopping distances
(Thinking distance plus braking distance)

Speed   Stopping distance

Thinking distance (m)
Braking distance (m)

(Average car length of a
family saloon – approx. 4 m)

20 mph   6 6 12 m
3 car lengths

30 mph   9 14 23 m
5 ¾ car lengths

40 mph   12 24 36 m
9 car lengths

50 mph   15 38 53 m
13 ¼ car lengths

60 mph   18 55 73 m
18 ¼ car lengths

70 mph   21 75 96 m
24 car lengths

THE HIGHWAY CODE SAYS:

- Drive at a speed that will allow you to stop well within the distance you can see to be clear.
- Leave enough space between you and the vehicle in front so that you can pull up safely if it suddenly slows down or stops.
- Drop back if someone overtakes and pulls into the gap in front of you.

EMERGENCY STOP

Even driving with normal care, you might have to stop abruptly, for instance if a pedestrian or vehicle suddenly appears in your path.

- Practise emergency stops in a quiet road with no following traffic.
- Remember that in an emergency you would not have time to signal or look in the mirror.
- If driving below the 30 mph speed limit, react instantly by pressing the foot brake and clutch pedal with both feet at once. Pressing the clutch prevents the engine stalling. At faster speeds, apply the foot brake first, pressing the clutch pedal just before stopping.
- Whatever your speed, press the foot brake down hard rather than stamping on it. That could make your car skid, especially on a wet road.
- Keep both hands on the wheel and steer straight to help prevent the wheels locking and causing a skid. For more on skidding see pp.154–5.

PARKING

- If possible, park off the road – e.g. in a car park.
- If you cannot park off the road, look out ahead for a roadside space where public parking is allowed and you do not inconvenience or endanger pedestrians or other road users. Try to park where you can stop on the left, with the passenger's door on the kerb side.

Normal parking

- Before pulling in, check your mirrors.
- At 25 mph, signal with your left indicator 50 m or so (about 55 yd) before your intended stop (much earlier at higher speeds). Practise using a left-turn arm signal too. Although arm signals are used less often these days, its extra emphasis can be useful.
- Slow down. If changing down through gears, shift into second gear.
- Pull in, stop and apply your handbrake.
- Switch off the engine and put the car into neutral gear.
- Stop signalling with your left indicator.
- Look behind your car before opening the driver's door.

Reverse parking

Backing into a parking space in a line of parked cars calls for extra skills.

- First indicate left, at the same time giving a left-turn arm signal.
- Stop beyond the space, with your car nearly 1 m (about 1 yd) out from the car parked beyond it. Your rear wheels should be about halfway along this parked car (**a**).
- Use your handbrake if necessary.

- Switch into reverse gear.
- Turn your head and look through your rear window.
- If another vehicle blocks your path backward, abandon the attempt and drive on until you find another parking space.
- Otherwise, release the handbrake and slowly reverse, slipping the clutch.
- With your left hand, pull the steering wheel down until your car's front offside is in line with the nearside headlight of the car parked behind your parking space (**b**). (You can first practise with no car behind the parking space.)

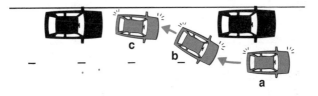

- Meanwhile, look forward to check that all is safe, for your car's offside front corner now sticks out into the road. Also watch for pedestrians stepping between you and the cars in front and behind you.
- With your left hand pull down harder on the steering wheel so your nearside rear wheel edges toward the kerb in the middle of the parking gap. Before the wheel touches, pull down hard on the steering wheel with your right hand to tuck the front of your car into the parking space (**c**). Take care that your car's nearside front corner clears the parked car in front.

- Before stopping, with your left hand pull down on the steering wheel to bring your car parallel to the kerb.
- If you are now more than one car-tyre width out from the kerb, manoeuvre slowly back and forth until you are closer but not touching the kerb.
- End midway between the cars in front and behind, leaving space for them to get out (**d**).

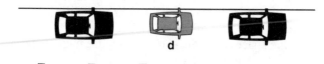

d

Parking on hills
- Park facing uphill in first gear, with the back of the front left wheel turned in to touch the kerb and the handbrake on (**e**).

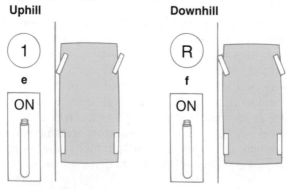

Uphill   **Downhill**

- Park facing downhill in reverse gear, with the front of the front left wheel turned in to touch the kerb and the handbrake on (**f**).

For advice on securing your car after parking, see p.213.

THE HIGHWAY CODE SAYS:

You must not stop or park:
- On the carriageway of a motorway.
- On a pedestrian crossing, including the area marked by the zig-zag lines.
- On a clearway.
- On an urban clearway within hours of operation except to pick up or set down passengers.
- In a road marked with double white lines even if one is broken, except to pick up or set down passengers.
- In a bus, tram or cycle lane during its hours of use.
- Where there are parking restrictions shown by yellow lines along the edge of the carriageway, or red lines along the edge of specially designated 'red routes'. The periods when restrictions apply are indicated by signs either adjacent to the kerb or on entry to a controlled parking zone.
- So as to endanger or inconvenience pedestrians or other road users – e.g. blocking wheelchair ramps.
- In a parking space reserved for specific users.
- At night facing oncoming traffic.
- On a road in fog, or at night without sidelights, except in a 30 mph speed limit and 10 m (11 yd) or more from a junction.

TURNING LEFT

Whenever making a turn, remember to check your
mirrors, signal, then make the manoeuvre
(mirror/signal/manoeuvre sequence).

Turning left into a minor road

To turn left off a main road into a minor road, follow
this sequence.

- If driving about 30 mph, check mirrors about 250 m
  (273 yd) in advance.
- Signal left with your indicator (**a**).
- Reduce speed.
- Change down to third gear.
- Brake lightly, if necessary.
- Change down to second gear and reach the turn-off

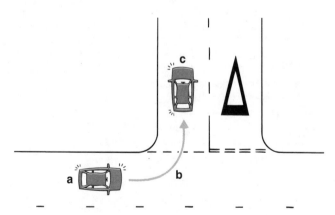

no faster than walking speed. Avoid the need for
sudden, last-moment braking.

- Check your mirrors.
- Glance over your left shoulder in case a cyclist or
  motorcyclist has crept up on your nearside.
- Beware pedestrians crossing the minor road or a wide
  load emerging from it.
- If your path is clear, steer around into the minor road,
  keeping about 1 m (about 1 yd) out (**b**). Do not cut
  the corner with your nearside front or rear wheel, or
  swing out across the minor road's centre line.
- Straighten up quickly and accelerate, changing back
  up through third gear to normal road speed, traffic
  permitting (**c**).
- Check your mirrors again.
- Cancel your left indicator if still signalling.

Turning left into a major road
To turn left from a minor road into a major road, follow
this sequence.

- Check mirrors, signal left, reduce speed and change
  down to third gear (**d** overleaf), as above.
- If there is a GIVE WAY sign and maybe a broken
  white line across the road or a triangle painted on it,
  approach the major road in second gear, ready to stop
  for traffic or to turn left (**e** overleaf) if your way is
  clear and you won't cause vehicles to slow or swerve.
- If there is a STOP sign you must stop at the major
  road even if no traffic is coming. Stop about 1 m
  (about 1 yd) from the left kerb, with the front of your
  car at the unbroken line where the minor road ends.
  Be sure to press the clutch pedal as you finish

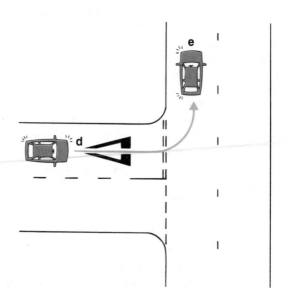

applying the foot brake. Engage first gear and apply
the handbrake if necessary.
- Whenever you reach a major road, keep looking out
  for pedestrians, cyclists and motorcylists. Give way
  to vehicles on the major road and pedestrians
  crossing your path.
- If parked vehicles limit your view, edge forward until
  you can see well both ways.
- Beware an approaching bus or truck that might hide
  an overtaking car. Beware a vehicle from the right
  which is signalling left. Its driver might have left an
  indicator on by mistake.

- If you have stopped, when the way ahead is clear, glance swiftly over your left shoulder for cyclists or motorcyclists on your left.
- If your way is still clear, turn left onto the major road, taking care not to clip the kerb.
- Quickly straighten up and accelerate, checking your mirrors as above.

THE HIGHWAY CODE SAYS:

- Take extra care at junctions. Check your position and speed. Junctions are particularly dangerous for cyclists, motorcyclists and pedestrians, so watch out for them before you turn. Watch out for long vehicles which may be turning at a junction ahead; they may have to use the whole width of the road to make the turn.
- Give way to pedestrians crossing a road into which you are turning.
- Well before you turn left, use your mirrors and give a left-turn sign. Do not overtake a cyclist, motorcyclist or horse rider immediately before turning left, and watch out for traffic coming up on your left before you make your turn. When turning, keep as close to the left as it is safe to do.
- If you want to turn left across a bus lane, cycle lane or tramway, give way to any vehicles using it from either direction.

TURNING RIGHT

Whenever making a turn, remember to follow the mirror/signal/manoeuvre sequence.

Turning right from a major road

- Check your mirrors well ahead of the turn.

- Signal right with your indicator (**a**).
- If another vehicle starts overtaking, let it.
- About 350 m (383 yd) before your turn-off, gently move toward the left centre of the road, getting into that position about 250 m (273 yd) before your turning.
- Start to let your speed slacken by now, then change down to third gear. You might also need to brake lightly.
- Change down to second gear about 40 m (44 yd) before your turning so as to reach it at a walking pace (**b**).
- Watch for oncoming vehicles, especially overtaking and two-wheeled vehicles. Beware wide loads

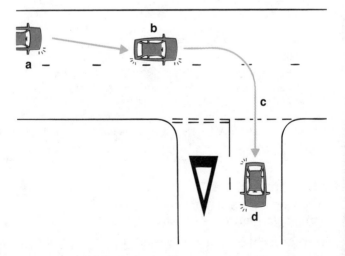

emerging from the minor road, or pedestrians crossing it.

- If your path is clear, turn right into the minor road without stopping (**c**).
- If your path is not clear, stop with the front of your car opposite the centre line of the minor road. (If you stop for more than a moment, you may choose to apply your handbrake and put your gear lever into neutral. Then, just before a safe gap in the oncoming traffic appears, engage first gear, keeping the clutch depressed, before moving off.) Check that your indicator still signals right. Glance in the mirrors, and quickly over your right shoulder in case a cyclist or motorcyclist has moved up alongside.
- Then, when your path is clear, turn right into the minor road, allowing extra time for an unexpected obstruction or an imperfect response from your car.
- Do not turn sharply enough to clip the 'wrong' side of the minor road.
- Straighten and accelerate, checking your mirrors (**d**).

Turning right into a major road

- Look out well ahead for road signs and markings.
- Check your mirrors.
- Signal right with your indicator (**e** overleaf).
- Reduce speed, changing down to third gear.
- Ease out until you are just left of the road's centre line.
- If there is a STOP sign ahead, stop with the front of your car at the line across your half of the road (**f** overleaf). (You may choose to apply the handbrake and put the gear lever into neutral.)

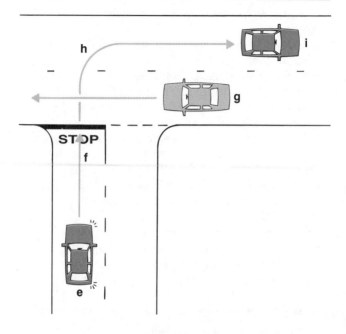

- Look both ways (remember to beware that a slow bus or truck might conceal a fast car overtaking it) and check your mirrors. If your field of view is quite narrow, wind down your window and listen for approaching traffic. At the last moment take a quick glance over your right shoulder.
- If you applied the handbrake earlier, now, when the road both ways is clear, engage first gear and let the clutch pedal rise to the biting point. Release the handbrake for a quick (but smooth) start.

- If pedestrians or vehicles (**g**) block your path at the last moment, stop. If necessary, change back into neutral, and apply the handbrake again.
- If there is a GIVE WAY instead of a STOP sign, change down to second gear about 30 m (33 yd) before the major road.
- If your path is clear in both directions, turn onto the major road without stopping.
- Whether you stopped or simply slowed down, drive straight across the major road, turning right only when you are at least halfway across (**h**).
- Straighten out, check your mirrors, stop indicating right, and accelerate to a safe speed (**i**).

THE HIGHWAY CODE SAYS:

- Well before you turn right, use your mirrors to make sure you know the position and movement of traffic behind you.
- Give a right-turn signal and, as soon as it is safe for you to do so, take up a position just left of the middle of the road or in the space marked for right-turning traffic. If possible leave room for other vehicles to pass on the left.
- Wait until there is a safe gap between you and any oncoming vehicle. Watch out for cyclists, motorcyclists and pedestrians; then make the turn, but do not cut the corner.
- Take great care when turning into a main road; you will need to watch for traffic in both directions and wait for a safe gap.

AT CROSSROADS
- Take special care at busy crossroads, as many road accidents happen here.
- Take special care at unmarked crossroads – e.g. in the back streets: do not assume you have the right of way.
- Take special care at crossroads where parked vehicles, vegetation or buildings limit your view.
- Look out well ahead for road signs and markings.
- Beware traffic turning, emerging or overtaking.
- Proceed only when it is safe to do so.

Driving straight across
If approaching from a minor road:
- Check your mirrors.
- Slow down in case you must stop.

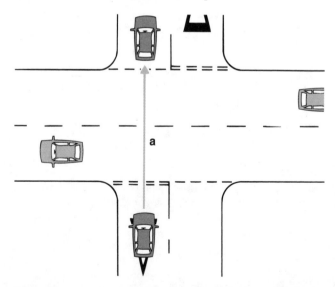

- If there are two marked lanes or room for them, normally you must get into the right-hand lane to let left-turning traffic behind you proceed. Follow the mirror/signal/manoeuvre sequence before doing so.
- Once in this lane do not signal right.
- Look in all directions as you approach the line across your side of the road.
- When it is safe, drive across the crossroads into the left-hand lane of the road opposite (**a**).

Turning left at crossroads
- Remember the mirror/signal/manoeuvre sequence.
- Treat this as you would a normal left turn (see pp.92–5), taking appropriate action depending on whether you turn from a major into a minor road or vice versa (**b**).

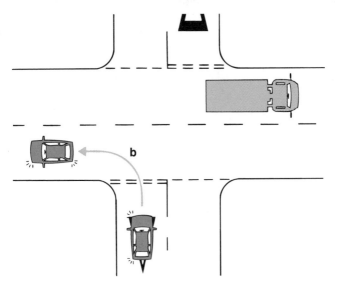

Turning right at crossroads

- Remember the mirror/signal/manoeuvre sequence.
- If turning from a major road into a minor road, normally steer right around and behind (**a**) the centre of a crossroads. An oncoming car turning right at the same time in the same way can then steer past you (**b**), and both cars will pass offside to offside.
- Sometimes an oncoming vehicle turning across your path, police traffic control, or road markings force you to turn so that both turning vehicles pass nearside to nearside (**c**). If so, beware oncoming vehicles hidden behind the one crossing your path.
- Be sure to drive slowly enough at crossroads to be able to stop if an oncoming vehicle crosses your path.
- In busy traffic, remember to leave room for oncoming vehicles to turn right, too.

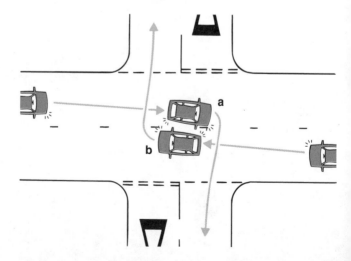

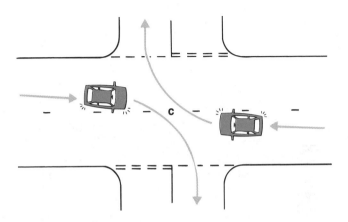

THE HIGHWAY CODE SAYS:

- When turning right at a junction where an oncoming vehicle is also turning right, it is normally safer to keep the other vehicle to your right and turn behind it – i.e. offside-to-offside. Before you complete the turn, check for other traffic on the road you want to cross.
- If the layout of the junction or the traffic situation makes offside-to-offside passing impracticable, pass nearside-to-nearside, but take care. The other vehicle could obstruct your view of the road so watch carefully for oncoming traffic.
- Box junctions have criss-cross yellow lines painted on the road. You MUST NOT enter the box until your exit road or lane from it is clear. But you may enter a box when you want to turn right and are only stopped from doing so by oncoming traffic or by vehicles waiting to turn right.

DUAL CARRIAGEWAYS

These may have two or three lanes each way, with a central reserve. There may be short additional lanes for vehicles leaving and entering. Remember that you may meet slow-moving bicycles and tractors on dual carriageways, although motorways ban these.

Turning left onto a dual carriageway

Enter as if turning left from a side road (**a**) unless there is a preliminary acceleration lane (**b**). If there is:

- Accelerate in second or third gear in the acceleration lane (**c**) to reach the same speed as the traffic in the left lane of the dual carriageway.
- Watch for a gap in the traffic in this lane.
- Check mirrors and glance quickly right to judge the speed and distance of vehicles behind the gap, but beware of merging vehicles ahead slowing down.
- Signal right and move into the gap (**d**).
- Stay in the left lane at first and cancel your signal.
- If your path is clear, you may move out to overtake. First check your mirrors and signal.
- After overtaking, return to the left lane when your path is clear. First check your mirrors and signal.

Turning left off a dual carriageway

If moving fast, plan manoeuvres well ahead.

- Be in the left-hand lane in plenty of time to turn off.
- Signal your left turn well in advance of the turn (**e**).
- Decelerate well in advance.
- If there is a deceleration lane leading to a slip road, move left into the deceleration lane (**f**).
- If there is no deceleration lane, turn off as if turning left onto a side road (**g**).

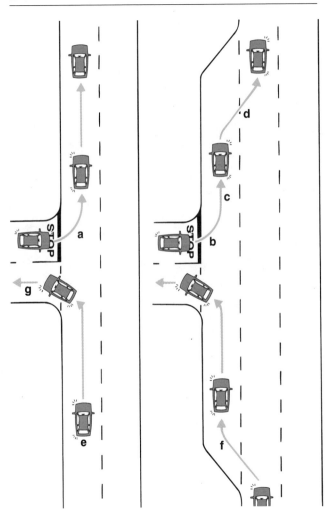

Turning right off a dual carriageway

- Watch for an arrowed deceleration lane leading to a gap in the central reserve.
- Follow the mirror/signal/manoeuvre sequence.
- If your path is clear, move into the deceleration lane at the start of the lane (**a**).
- Slow down.
- If there is oncoming traffic, wait in the gap in the central reserve until your way is clear (**b**). Be sure to

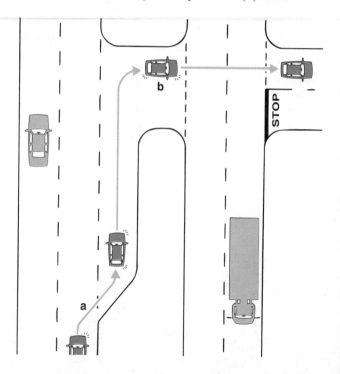

stop opposite the left lane of the road you want to
turn into so that you drive straight into this without
obstructing traffic coming out of its right lane.

Turning right onto a dual carriageway

This involves crossing the dual carriageway at a gap in
the central reserve and turning right into the left-hand
lane on the far side.

- Stop and wait until you can cross to the gap in the
  central reserve without making vehicles already on
  the dual carriageway slow or swerve (**c**).
- If the gap in the central reserve is clear and large
  enough to take the length of your vehicle, you may
  stop there until you can safely continue across (**d**).
- If the gap in the middle is not clear or is too short to
  stop in, you must wait until the dual carriageway is
  clear in both directions.
- Once the way is clear, turn smoothly (**e**).

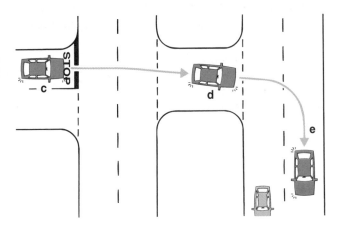

THE HIGHWAY CODE SAYS:

- When going straight across or turning right into a dual carriageway, treat each half as a separate road. Wait in the central reserve until there is a safe gap in the traffic on the second half of the road. If the central reserve is too narrow for the length of your vehicle, wait until you can cross both carriageways in one go.
- When turning right from a dual carriageway, wait in the opening in the central reserve until you are sure it is safe to cross the other half of the carriageway.

ROUNDABOUTS

These include large and small (mini-roundabout) circular islands where several roads meet. Roundabouts let traffic move smoothly from one road to another, usually without stopping. Vehicles circulate clockwise around them, using the appropriate lane for their exit, unless road markings or signs indicate otherwise. What follows is based on three lanes, but some roundabouts have more than three.

Approaching a roundabout

- Change down, usually through third to second gear.
- Check your mirrors.
- If necessary, signal and change lanes.
- Prepare to stop at the broken line across the road where you enter the roundabout if your way ahead is not clear.
- Beware traffic crossing your path.
- Give way to vehicles entering from your right unless road markings show otherwise.

Turning left at a roundabout

- Signalling left, approach in the left-hand lane (**a**).
- Stay in that lane on the way round the roundabout (**b**).
- Keep signalling left until you have turned off (**c**).

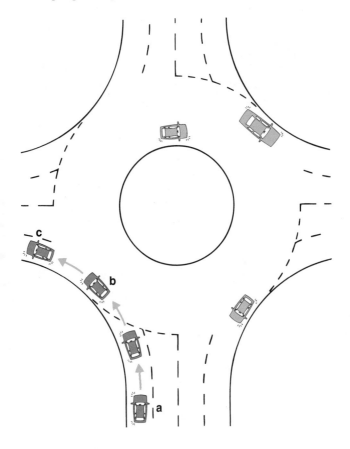

Turning right at a roundabout

- Signalling right, approach in the right-hand lane (**a**).
- Stay in that lane on the way round the roundabout (**b**). You will be moving across lanes, so be sure before entering the roundabout that all lanes are clear to your right.
- Keep signalling right.
- Check your mirrors, especially for vehicles coming up on your left.
- While passing the turn-off before the one you want, start signalling left (**c**). If your path is clear, move into the left lane.

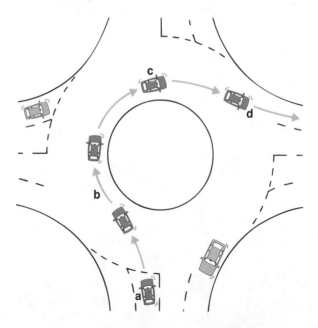

- If your path is clear, turn off (**d**).
- Stop signalling.

Going straight on at a roundabout

- Approach in the left-hand lane without signalling (**e**).
- Stay in that lane as you go round the roundabout (**f**).
- Check your mirrors, especially for vehicles coming up on your left.
- While passing the turn-off before the one you want, start signalling left (**g**).
- If your path is clear, turn off (**h**).
- Stop signalling.

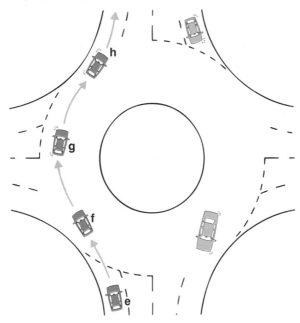

THE HIGHWAY CODE SAYS:

- Watch out for traffic crossing in front of you on the roundabout, especially vehicles intending to leave by the next exit. Show them consideration.
- Watch out for motorcyclists, cyclists and horse riders. Give them plenty of room.
- Long vehicles may have to take a different course, both approaching and on the roundabout. Watch for signals.
- The same rules apply to mini-roundabouts as to roundabouts. If possible, pass around the central marking. Watch out for vehicles making U-turns and for long vehicles which may have to cross the centre of the mini-roundabout.

TRAFFIC LIGHTS

Traffic lights control traffic at certain road junctions and roadworks. Special traffic lights control traffic at airports and bridges.

- Ordinary traffic lights show red, amber and green in sequence.
- Other traffic lights show flashing red lights.
- Flashing amber lights warn of a school crossing point.

Sequence of lights

Learn the sequence of lights, and what each part of the sequence means, by studying the Highway Code and watching traffic lights in operation.

1 Red. Stop behind the stop line.

2 Red and amber. Stop and wait. Be ready to go.

3 Green. Go if the road is clear.

4 Amber. Stop unless you have passed the stop line or

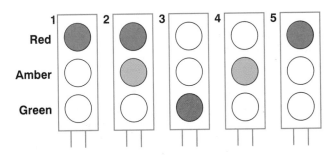

are so near that stopping might cause another vehicle to crash into you.

5 Red again. Stop behind the stop line.

Approaching traffic lights

- Look out for these well ahead.
- Keep your speed low enough to stop if necessary when you reach traffic lights, especially if these were already green when you first saw them.
- If several lanes are marked on the road, use your mirrors, signal and, when safe to do so, move into the lane you want, slowing and changing down. If intending to go straight ahead, beware the right-hand lane if there is a vehicle ahead of you, even if an arrow shows you may use that lane. When the lights go green the vehicle might be kept waiting to turn right.
- If the lights turn green when you are less than 200 m (219 yd) away they are unlikely to turn amber before you arrive. In such cases, 25 mph is normally a safe approach speed.
- If a set of traffic lights shows a green filter arrow you

may proceed in that direction if you want to, even if a
main light is showing red. Leave room for cyclists.

● If the lights have failed, stop to check that your path
is clear and carry on cautiously, as if at an ordinary
road junction.

Waiting at traffic lights

● When you stop at a red light or an amber light that
follows green, apply the handbrake and put your gear
into neutral.

● When you stop at a red/amber light, keep your car in
first gear and your foot on the foot brake, ready to
move off.

● Keep an eye on your mirrors.

● When the cross flow of traffic ahead stops, change
into first gear, ready to move off.

● Do not move off until the green light appears.

Moving off

● Before moving off make sure no pedestrian or
crosswise traffic is still crossing your path.

● If you are about to turn left or right, make sure you do
not knock down a cyclist or motorcyclist who has
moved up along one side of you.

● If oncoming traffic blocks your right turn, follow the
procedure described for junctions (p.102).

THE HIGHWAY CODE SAYS:

● You MUST obey all traffic light signals and traffic signs
giving orders. Make sure you also know and act on all
other traffic signs and road markings.

● At junctions controlled by traffic lights you MUST stop

behind the white stop line across your side of the road
unless the light is green. You MUST NOT move forward
when the red and amber lights are showing.
● Do not go forward when the traffic lights are green
unless there is room for you to clear the junction safely
or you are taking up a position to turn right.

ONE-WAY SYSTEMS
These usually comprise two or more lanes for vehicles
moving in one direction.
● Memorize the no-entry sign for vehicular traffic (**a**).

a

● Never drive the wrong way up a one-way street.
● Follow markings dividing the street into lanes.
● In a multi-lane one-way system, vehicles may drive
in and overtake in any lane so make frequent use of
your mirrors to check what is happening behind you.
● Before making a lane change check your mirrors,
glance back, signal and recheck. Change lanes only
when it is safe.
● If changing lanes, give way to drivers already in the
lane to which you are moving.
● Get in the lane you will need long before the one-way
street ends.

- If you intend turning left, get into the left-hand lane (**b**).
- If you intend going straight ahead, get into the centre lane if there is one (**c**).
- If you intend turning right, get into the right-hand lane if it is free from parked vehicles or other obstructions (**d**).
- Watch out for unwary drivers in vehicles entering the right-hand lane from roads to the right.
- If in doubt, stick to the lane you first entered.

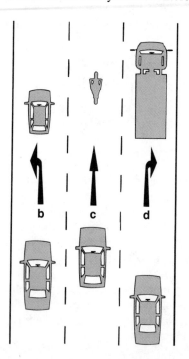

- If you leave lane-changing too late, do not cut across busy traffic and risk an accident. Drive on until you find an alternative route to the road that you want.

THE HIGHWAY CODE SAYS:

- In one-way streets, choose the correct lane for your exit as soon as you can. Do not change lanes suddenly.
- Unless road signs or markings indicate otherwise, choose the left-hand lane when going to the left, the right-hand lane when going to the right and the most appropriate lane when going straight ahead.
- Remember – traffic could be passing on both sides.

TURNING AROUND

Drivers needing to turn a vehicle around on the road to face the opposite way can do so in one of four ways.

Turning in the road using forward and reverse gears
This involves turning across a road in three or more stages, trying not to stick out over the kerbs. Perform this only on a quiet side-road that is wide enough and free from obstructions such as parked cars, lampposts and passing pedestrians.

- Using the mirror/signal/manoeuvre sequence, pull over to the left (**a** overleaf).
- Apply the handbrake, putting the gear lever in neutral.
- Press down on the clutch and engage first gear.
- Check mirrors and glance right over your shoulder.
- When all is clear, release the handbrake and move off at a crawl, turning your steering wheel as far to the right as you can.

- Straighten up to approach the right-hand kerb head on.
- At the last moment, turn the steering wheel hard to the left (**b**).
- Meanwhile, look both ways for approaching traffic.
- Press down on the foot brake and clutch pedals so as to stop just before your front wheels touch the kerb, and apply the handbrake.
- Engage reverse gear.
- Check for traffic in all directions.
- If all is clear, reverse slowly, looking back over your left shoulder.
- As your vehicle's rear end approaches the opposite kerb (**c**), look over your right shoulder and turn the steering wheel hard right.
- Press down on the foot brake and clutch pedals to stop just before your vehicle's rear end reaches the kerb, and apply the handbrake.
- Check for traffic in all directions.
- When it is safe to go, drive off in first gear, straightening up on the left-hand side of the road (**d**).

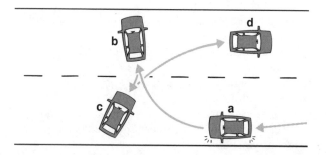

- If you still cannot clear the opposite kerb, reverse once more.

Reversing into a side road on your left

Instead of turning in the road, you can reverse into a quiet side road. Never reverse into a main road. (For reversing technique, see pp.51–2.)

- Using the mirror/signal/manoeuvre sequence, drive just past a side road to your left and stop by the kerb, parallel to it (**a**).
- Check all around for vehicles and pedestrians.
- If it is safe reverse very slowly around the corner into the side road, close to the kerb, and stop (**b**). Get someone to give you visual help if you cannot see

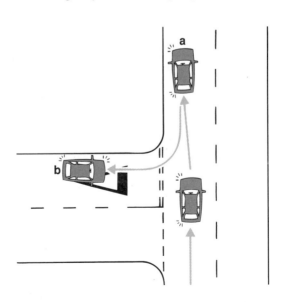

your way clearly, and be prepared to stop and give
way to vehicles or to pedestrians crossing the road.
- Reverse no farther than necessary.
- When your way is clear, signal and drive forward
  slowly. Then turn right into the road you were on
  originally, so that you are now going in the opposite
  direction (**c**).

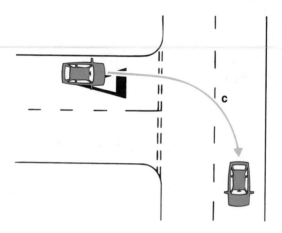

Reversing into a side road on your right

This might be necessary if you cannot find a side road
on your left, or you lack a clear view through the rear
window (in a van, for example).
- Using the mirror/signal/manoeuvre sequence, pull
  over to the right-hand side of the road just past a
  suitable side road on the right and stop by the kerb,
  parallel to it (**a**).

- Look all around for traffic and pedestrians. Watch out especially for oncoming vehicles.
- If it is safe, reverse very slowly around the corner into the side road, close to the kerb, and stop (**b**). As you go, check nearness to the kerb by looking over your right shoulder, but also continue looking in all directions.
- When your way is clear, signal left and drive forward and across the side road into the left-hand lane (**c**).

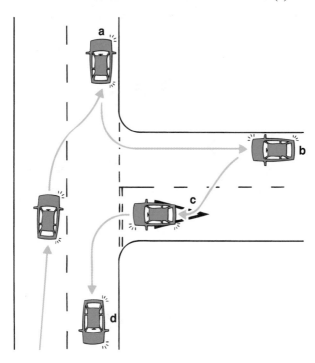

You can now turn left into the road you were on
originally so that you are going in the opposite
direction (**d** on previous page).

Making a U-turn
This involves turning a vehicle around in the road in
one movement, without stopping to reverse. Only
attempt it on very quiet, broad roads.
- Check that the road is clear in both directions, using
  your mirrors and glancing back briefly.
- Slow down to walking speed, keeping well to the left,
  and signal right (**a**).
- Repeat your visual checks.

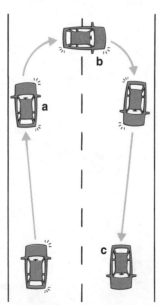

- If your way is clear, turn your steering wheel hard to the right and make your U-turn at a walking pace (**b**).
- Straighten up on the left-hand side of the road and accelerate, checking your mirror and cancelling your indicator (**c**). Do not drive over the kerb.
- Do not attempt a U-turn if you are not sure the road is wide enough.
- If making a U-turn at a mini-roundabout, beware other vehicles. Their drivers will not expect it.
- Never attempt this manoeuvre in one-way streets, on motorways, or where road signs forbid it.

See pp.51–2 for general rules on reversing and reversing straight back.

THE HIGHWAY CODE SAYS:

- Before reversing make sure there are no pedestrians – particularly children – or obstructions in the road behind you.
- Be aware of the 'blind spot' behind you – the part of the road that is obscured from the driving seat.
- Reverse with care. If you cannot see clearly, get someone to guide you.
- You MUST NOT reverse your vehicle for longer than necessary.
- NEVER reverse from a side road into a main road.
- Avoid reversing into the road from a driveway; where possible, reverse in and drive out in forward position.

WEARING SEAT BELTS

The driver and adult passengers are individually
responsible for wearing seat belts and must do so if
belts are available, unless medically exempt. The driver
is responsible for seeing that children wear appropriate
safety devices as shown in the table below.

Safety devices for children

Age/height of child	Front seat device	Rear seat device
Children under 1 year of age	Approved baby carrier suitable for child's weight	Baby carrier with seat belt or carrycot restrained by straps
Children aged 1–3	Appropriate child restraint or seat belt	Appropriate child restraint or booster seat used with seat belt
Children aged 4–13 (under 1.5 m tall)	Appropriate child restraint or seat belt	Appropriate child restraint or seat belt
Children aged 14 and over (over 1.5 m tall)	Seat belt	Seat belt if available

Child seat

THE HIGHWAY CODE SAYS:

- Wearing seat belts saves lives and reduces the risks of serious injury in an accident. You MUST wear a seat belt if one is available, unless you are exempt.
- An appropriate child restraint is a baby carrier, child seat, harness or booster seat appropriate to the child's weight.
- Do not let children sit behind the rear seats in an estate car or hatchback. Make sure that child safety door locks, where fitted, are used when children are in the car. Keep children under control in the car.

MOTORWAY DRIVING

A motorway has four or more lanes, half carrying
traffic one way, the rest the opposite way, with a central
reserve between. The hard shoulder is only for vehicles
that break down. Motorways are meant for safe, fast
driving. This calls for total alertness and plenty of fast-
traffic experience.

Learners and slow-moving vehicles must not use
motorways, but the driving test examiner may ask
motorway questions, and advance knowledge prepares
learners for what to expect when they are qualified to
drive on these fast multi-lane roads.

Before you drive on a motorway

- Study the Highway Code's sections on motorway
  driving.
- Memorize the motorway signs and signals.
- Get advice from a professional instructor.
- Observe motorway driving as a passenger.
- Only drive on a motorway when fully ready.
- Make sure all your car's systems are working.
- Practise on less busy stretches of motorway.
- Practise keeping up with traffic flowing along at
  60–70 mph.
- Before a long journey fill up with fuel, oil and water.
- Check that any load is secure.
- Do not enter a motorway feeling ill or tired – you
  may not stop on a motorway except in an emergency,
  and exits and service areas can be far apart.
- On a long journey, make sure to let plenty of fresh air
  into the car to prevent drowsiness.

Traffic joining a motorway

There are three places for joining a motorway:

1 Where a main road widens to become a motorway.

2 Where a motorway starts at a roundabout.

3 Where a slip road leads to an acceleration lane
   joining a motorway. On this lane adapt your speed to
   the motorway traffic flow before slotting into a space
   in the left-hand motorway lane (**a**).

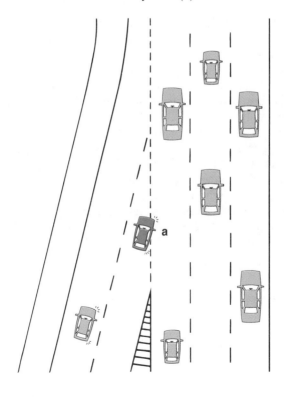

Motorway lane discipline

- Drive in the left-hand lane unless overtaking or unless it holds many vehicles slower than you.
- Look far ahead, allowing extra time to anticipate problems and take safe, appropriate action.
- Leave a long braking space between you and the vehicle ahead.
- When changing lanes, begin your mirror/signal/ manoeuvre sequence earlier than usual to take account of high motorway speeds.
- After overtaking, move back in. Do not hold up vehicles faster than yours – even if they are breaking the 70 mph motorway speed limit.
- Watch out for roadworks with temporary speed limits, lane closures and contraflow systems.
- Do not move to the left to overtake.
- Only overtake on the hard shoulder if traffic signs or police officers tell you to.
- Where vehicles are joining the motorway from an acceleration lane, prepare to reduce speed to let them in, or move right if it is safe.
- Notice overhead direction signs, and change lanes in good time if you need to.
- To leave a motorway before it ends, allow plenty of time to move from the left-hand lane into the deceleration lane leading to the slip road.

THE HIGHWAY CODE SAYS:

- When you join the motorway, you MUST give way to traffic already on the motorway. Adjust your speed so that you join the left-hand lane where there is a safe gap and at the same speed as traffic in that lane.

- After joining the motorway, stay in the left-hand lane long enough to get used to the speed of traffic before overtaking.
- When you can see well ahead and the road conditions are good, drive at a steady cruising speed. Keep a safe distance from the vehicle in front and increase the gap on wet or icy roads, or in fog.
- You MUST NOT stop except in an emergency or when told to do so by the police, by an emergency sign or by flashing red light signals.
- If you break down, pull onto the hard shoulder and stop as far to the left as possible. Leave the vehicle by the left-hand door and walk to an emergency telephone. After telephoning for help, wait near your vehicle but well away from the carriageway and hard shoulder. If you feel at risk, get into your vehicle by a left-hand door and lock all doors.
- You MUST NOT reverse, cross the central reserve, or drive against the traffic flow. Even if you have missed your exit, or have taken the wrong route, carry on to the next exit.
- Watch for the signs letting you know you are getting near your exit. If you are not already in the left-hand lane, move into it well before reaching your exit and stay in it. Signal left in good time and slow down as necessary.
- Check your speedometer and adjust your speed accordingly.

4. Special situations

SAFE DRIVING

Safe driving involves planning ahead to cope safely
with all situations. If you stick to this principle, you
should be able to cope with even the trickiest situation.
This chapter starts with general principles of safe
driving, followed by particular problems.

The keys to safe driving are:

- Being aware of everything you can see on the road.
- Anticipating other road users' actions, including
  errors and even aggressive behaviour.
- Always keeping control of your vehicle.
- Thinking before you act.
- Showing patience, consideration and courtesy for
  other road users, including pedestrians.
- Avoiding hostile or competitive behaviour likely to
  annoy or endanger other road users.
- Knowing and practising the Highway Code.

HAZARDS

Anything that makes you alter speed or course is a
hazard. Be prepared to cope with all possible hazards
ahead.

Anticipating hazards

- Stay alert, observant and ready to react to any hazard
  you meet.
- Look far ahead.
- Keep looking in your mirrors to check what is behind.
- Watch for hints of problems about to arise.

Hints of hazards ahead

Signs of likely hazards ahead can include:

- Sharp bends (**a**).
- Road junctions (**b**).
- Roadworks (**c**).
- Road signs.
- Vehicles indicating making a turn: they might have forgotten to switch off their indicators (**d**).
- Parked vehicles, especially those with a driver and emitting exhaust vapour: they might be about to move off (**e**).

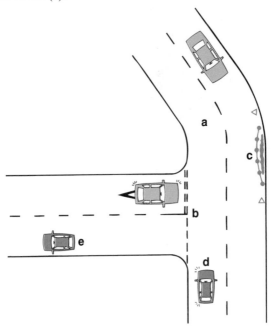

- Oncoming vehicles overtaking (**f**).
- Cyclists and motorcyclists (**g**).
- Pedestrians, especially children at play, the old or infirm, and anyone about to cross a road (**h**).
- Horse riders.
- Dogs or other animals not under control.
- Big lorries (**i**): they need extra stopping space and might have to swing far out to the left or right to turn at a roundabout, crossroads or factory gate.

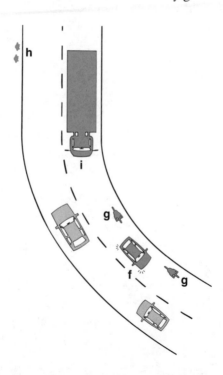

Driving defensively

Allow time and distance to react to each hazard as it arises. Here are general rules you should always obey.

- Drive at a safe speed for the conditions.
- Give appropriate signals.
- Be able to stop safely behind the vehicle ahead if it suddenly brakes.
- On a narrow road, be able to stop behind a parked vehicle to let an oncoming vehicle past.
- Drive in the appropriate gear for your speed and the road and traffic conditions.
- Drive in the appropriate position on the road.
- Overtake as quickly as possible.
- Let other drivers overtake you if they wish, even if they exceed the speed limit.
- Do not drive too close when overtaking cyclists or parked cars.
- Do not overtake on the left except in a one-way system, a slow-moving queue or if it is safe and the vehicle ahead has signalled a right-hand turn.
- Avoid changing lanes without reason.
- Do not obstruct 'Keep Clear' road markings at junctions.
- Watch out for cyclists and motorcyclists overtaking on your left at a junction.
- Give way to pedestrians crossing the road in front of you when stopped at a junction.
- Never assume that other drivers and road users will behave in a proper, responsible way.
- If other road users' errors interfere with your progress, reduce speed or stop, even if it is your right of way.

Reacting to hazards

Each time you identify a hazard you should respond with the mirror/signal/manoeuvre sequence.

- Look in your mirrors to check what is following and how far back.
- If you intend to slow down or change course, give the appropriate signal in plenty of time.
- In good time, position your vehicle in the appropriate lane early enough to tackle the hazard without interfering with other road users.
- Be ready to slow down and stop when you reach the hazard, in case there are problems.
- If you can safely do so, perform your manoeuvre.
- All the time watch for problems ahead, and look in all directions if you come to a junction. Here, obstructions can include traffic turning and pedestrians crossing.

TRAFFIC AHEAD

Keep a close watch on the road ahead, and at junctions look in both directions.

- Leave at least a two-second gap between your vehicle and the one ahead.
- At least double this gap in poor weather.
- Scan the road in front, assessing the traffic and preparing for problems – for instance an obstruction caused by a parked lorry on the left and an oncoming car overtaking a cyclist (**a**).
- Watch out for bends. Adjust speed and position to take account of a sharp bend and its camber.
- Watch out for junctions.
- Where roads meet be sure you can see and be seen

by other road users. Look out for pedestrians, cyclists and motorcyclists obscured by parked vehicles.

- Where parked vehicles or other obstructions limit your view at a junction with a main road, before joining this, creep slowly forward to widen your field of view, using visual clues such as vehicles reflected in shop windows or glimpsed through parked cars' windows.

TRAFFIC BEHIND

Using your mirrors, keep a close watch on the road
behind. You might affect following traffic if you have
to change speed or direction.

- Look behind your car before opening a door, moving
  off, overtaking, changing lanes, changing direction,
  turning, slowing or stopping.
- Watch out for vehicles likely to overtake you.
- If a vehicle crowds up closely behind, slow down
  slightly to widen the gap between you and the vehicle
  ahead, giving you more stopping distance and the
  driver behind a chance to overtake.
- Glance over your shoulder to see traffic (**a**) hidden by
  your mirrors' blind spots before you change lanes or
  where traffic merges from two lanes or roads.
- Notice the positions and speed of following vehicles
  and try to predict their drivers' actions. Take what you
  see into account before signalling and manoeuvring.

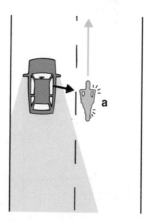

GREEN AND FAULTY TRAFFIC LIGHTS

Traffic lights showing green as you approach, or traffic lights that are not working, should be treated as hazards, not as invitations to drive on regardless of traffic conditions.

Lights showing green

Quickly sum up the situation if you approach traffic lights showing green, and prepare to react.

- Lights set at green when you first saw them might be about to change colour. Change down through the gears on approach in case you need to stop.
- If vehicles are already queuing on crosswise roads, the lights might change colour at any moment. Again, change down through the gears on approach in case you need to stop.
- Do not accelerate, hoping to squeeze across. You could hit a vehicle starting from another road (**a**).

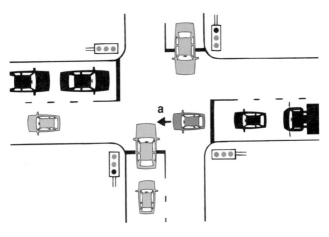

- Drive at a speed at which you can stop safely if the lights change.
- Do not rely on having to brake suddenly. You might skid or be hit by a following vehicle.
- If a big lorry is behind you, allow for the long stopping distance the lorry will need.

Lights not working

If traffic lights controlling a crossroads are not working, drive with great care. Treat the junction as an unmarked crossroads.

NARROW ROADS

Take special care on roads too narrow for passing or overtaking except at short wider sections to the left or the right.

- Watch out ahead, allowing time to stop.
- Slow down when you cannot see around a bend.
- If you see an oncoming car, stop in a passing place on the left to let it by (**a**), or opposite a passing place on the right until the car lets you by.
- Use a passing place to let a following vehicle by if its driver wishes to overtake you.

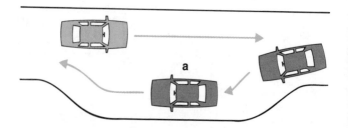

THE HIGHWAY CODE SAYS:

- Some roads (often called single-track roads) are only wide enough for one vehicle. They may have special passing places.
- Pull into a passing place on your left, or wait opposite a passing place on your right, when you see a vehicle coming towards you, or if the driver behind you wants to overtake.
- Give way to vehicles coming uphill whenever you can.
- Do not park in passing places.

PEDESTRIANS AND ANIMALS

Pedestrians and animals, as well as motor vehicles, have the right to use roads. Drivers must show them consideration and make special allowance for unexpected behaviour.

Giving way to pedestrians

- Stop at zebra crossings in use and at pelican crossings when a red light shows.
- Give way to pedestrians crossing pelican crossings when an amber light flashes.
- Prepare to give way to pedestrians waiting to cross a zebra crossing.
- Do not overtake on a pedestrian crossing or its approaches marked on the road.
- When driving out of one road into another watch out for pedestrians and give way to any crossing your path.
- When driving past vehicles parked in a narrow road, drive slowly and leave a gap between you and them in case a pedestrian steps out between them.

- Allow for slow reactions by elderly people.
- Allow for children running out into the road from behind vehicles such as ice-cream vans, school buses or lorries (**a**).
- Allow for the fact that pedestrians with poor sight or hearing might not see or hear you coming.

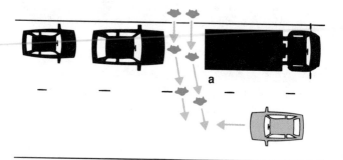

Watching for animals on the road

- Slow down when approaching a horse on the road. Be ready to stop if the horse becomes nervous.
- Stop and switch off the engine if someone with animals signals that you should stop.
- Give animals a wide berth when you pass and drive past them quietly and slowly.
- If you injure a dog, horse, cow, donkey, mule, goat, pig or sheep with your vehicle you must stop and give your name and address and vehicle registration number to anyone with a reason to ask for them. If no one is there to take your details, you must report to the police within 24 hours.

THE HIGHWAY CODE SAYS:

- Show consideration to pedestrians. Drive carefully and slowly when there are pedestrians about, especially in crowded shopping streets or residential areas and near bus and tram stops, parked milk floats or mobile shops. Watch out for pedestrians emerging suddenly into the road, especially from behind parked vehicles.
- Watch out for children and elderly pedestrians who may not be able to judge your speed and could step into the road in front of you. Watch out for blind and partially sighted people who may be carrying white sticks (white with two red reflective bands for deaf and blind people) or using guide dogs, and for people with other disabilities. Give them plenty of time to cross the road. Do not assume that all pedestrians can hear your vehicle coming; they may have hearing difficulties.
- Drive slowly near schools. In some places, there is a flashing amber signal below the 'School' warning sign which tells you that there may be children crossing the road ahead. When these signals are flashing, drive very slowly until you are well clear of the area. Drive carefully when passing a stationary bus showing a 'School Bus' sign; children may be getting on or off.
- You MUST stop when a school crossing patrol shows a 'Stop–Children' sign.
- Be careful near parked ice-cream vans.
- At road junctions give way to pedestrians who are already crossing the road into which you are turning.
- In a queue of traffic, you MUST keep pedestrian crossings clear.
- At pedestrian crossings controlled by lights, give way to pedestrians who are still crossing after the vehicles' signal has changed to green.

- Give way to pedestrians on a pavement you need to cross, e.g. to reach a driveway.
- Be prepared for pedestrians walking in the road, especially on narrow country roads. Give them plenty of room. Take extra care on left-hand bends and keep your speed down.
- Watch out for animals being led or ridden on the road and take extra care at left-hand bends and on narrow country roads. Drive slowly past animals. Give them plenty of room and be ready to stop. Do not scare animals by sounding your horn or revving your engine.
- Look out for horse riders' signals and be aware that they may not move to the centre of the road prior to turning right. Riders of horses and ponies are often children – so take extra care.

CYCLISTS AND MOTORCYCLISTS

Cyclists and motorcyclists also have road rights. Bicycles and motorcycles are less stable and less easily seen than cars and are more vulnerable to poor road surfaces. Bicycles also move much slower than most other road users. Always be on the lookout for both, and treat them with care.

Coping with cyclists

Treat a cyclist the same as a small car. When overtaking, leave plenty of space (more than a car door's width) in case a cyclist:

- Swerves to avoid a drain cover or pothole (**a**).
- Wobbles in a crosswind.
- Veers aside to cross rails set in the road.
- Weaves to and fro or dismounts, going uphill.

High-risk situations

- At junctions always look out for cyclists and
  motorcyclists who are:
  - Hidden by other vehicles.
  - Coming up on your inside before you turn left.
- At dusk and dawn beware cyclists and motorcyclists
  who are riding without lights.

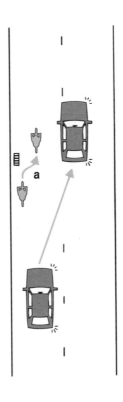

DAMP AND WET WEATHER

Condensation inside windows and rain on their outside surfaces affect visibility. Water on roads reduces tyre grip and so affects steering and braking. Act to reduce the risks that result.

Keeping glass clear

Always be ready for condensation and rain.

- Regularly clean the windscreen, windows, lights and mirrors.
- Regularly top up your washer bottle.
- Regularly check windscreen blades and replace if worn.
- Keep a dry cloth inside the car for wiping condensation off windows before you start.

Driving in the wet

- Switch on demisters and window heaters to keep windows free of condensation.
- If necessary, open windows to remove condensation.
- Drive through rain using dipped headlights (use these also in gloomy dry weather).
- Reduce speed if your wipers cannot work fast enough to keep the windscreen clear in a downpour or from spray thrown up by other vehicles.
- Reduce speed in rain on poorly lit roads at night.
- In rain allow twice the usual braking distance.
- Turn corners with care on wet roads, especially when they are oily after dry weather.
- Look out for water on the road.
- Decelerate (do not brake) if your steering seems suddenly light. Your car may be aquaplaning: its tyres sliding along on a skin of water between them

and the road. In such cases, you risk losing all
steering and braking control.

- Beware of driving through a deep puddle in the side
  of the road. Your nearside wheels will slow down,
  making you swerve (**a**).
- Pass pedestrians slowly enough not to drench them
  with spray.
- Beware of driving through roads flooded deep
  enough for water to splash up into your car's
  electrical equipment, making it stall.
- Cross flooded roads slowly in first gear with a high
  engine speed by pressing the clutch pedal gently
  down and up. Avoid throwing up a wave which might
  stop the car engine working.
- Check your brakes by pumping the brake pedal
  gently after passing through water.

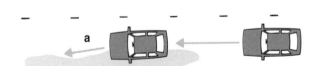

FOG

The main danger in fog is not seeing vehicles ahead of
you; especially if driving too fast, you might crash into
a vehicle ahead when it slows or stops. Shunting
accidents can involve dozens of vehicles, killing and
injuring numbers of people, especially on dual
carriageways and motorways.

In very foggy conditions, do not travel by car at all if you can avoid it. Delay your journey instead, or try to find a safer method of travel.

Preparing for fog

If driving is unavoidable, make it as safe as you possibly can.

- Check that all your lights work.
- Make sure you will be able to see ahead as far as possible, and that other road users will be able to see you. Do the following before setting out:
  - If your windscreen is misted up inside, wipe it dry with a cloth or paper towel before driving, and direct hot air to the windscreen with the fan full on.
  - Wipe other windows and mirrors if they are also misted up.
  - Switch on windscreen wipers to keep the outside of the windscreen clear.
  - Switch on headlamps, using dipped beams. Do not use main beams. These can restrict vision and dazzle other road users.
  - Use fog lamps if you have them. Switch on powerful rear fog lamps only if visibility falls below 100 m (109 yd). Otherwise, they might dazzle following drivers. Switch off when fog clears.
- Allow extra time for your journey.

Driving in fog

- Be aware of the weather. Expect fog if it is mentioned on weather forecasts or signalled by roadside signs.

- If fog threatens, try to avoid motorways and dual
  carriageways, where the worst pile-ups happen in
  foggy weather.
- Beware fog patches on the road ahead (**a**).

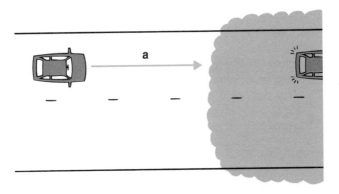

- If you enter fog, slow down.
- If you find you are following another vehicle in fog,
  drop back.
- Keep well behind any vehicle you are following. If
  you can see its tail lights in dense fog you are
  probably driving too close.
- Drive slowly enough to be able to stop safely within
  the distance that you can see to be clear. This might
  mean driving at walking pace.
- Allow extra stopping space if the road is wet or
  slippery.
- Do not try to keep up with the vehicle ahead if you
  judge its speed is too high for safety.
- Do not attempt to overtake in fog. The chances are

you cannot see as far ahead as you think you can.

- Ignore risk-takers who overtake you.
- In patchy fog, resist the temptation to drive fast in clear gaps between foggy patches.

Finding the way

- Make the most of road markings to help you keep a safe position on the road. These include reflective 'cat's eyes':
  - White 'cat's eyes' indicate the middle of a road or show lane boundaries.
  - Red 'cat's eyes' on some roads show the left-hand edge.
  - Green 'cat's eyes' mark lay-bys and slip roads.
  - A dual carriageway may have amber 'cat's eyes' between the right-hand lane and central reserve.
- Beware confusing a line marking the road centre with a lane boundary line.
- Drive in the middle of your lane or your side of the road if that is not divided into lanes.
- Do not straddle the centre line or hug it too closely. Oncoming traffic might hit you.

Stopping in fog

- If you break down, switch on your hazard lights as you pull over.
- Keep your hazard lights switched on while you are stopped.
- Notify the police or recovery service. (See also Breakdowns, pp. 159–61.)
- If your broken-down car obstructs traffic, have it removed as quickly as you can.

- Try to find a suitable place to park off the road.
- If you must park on the road, leave side lights on.

THE HIGHWAY CODE SAYS:

- Make sure your windscreen, windows and lights are clean and that all your lights (including brake lights) are working.
- When driving in fog, see and be seen. If you cannot see clearly, use dipped headlights. Use front or rear fog lights if visibility is seriously reduced but switch them off when visibility improves. Use your windscreen wipers and demisters.
- Check your mirrors and slow down. Keep a safe distance behind the vehicle in front. You should always be able to pull up within the distance you can see clearly.
- Do not try to keep the tail lights of the vehicle in front in clear view; it gives a false sense of security.
- Be aware of your speed; you may be going much faster than you think. Do not accelerate to get away from a vehicle that is too close behind you. When you slow down, use your brakes so that your brake lights warn drivers behind you.
- When the word 'Fog' is shown on a roadside signal but the road appears to be clear, be prepared for a bank of fog or drifting smoke ahead. Even if it seems to be clearing, you can suddenly find yourself back in thick fog.
- It is especially dangerous to park on the road in fog. If it is unavoidable, leave your side lights on.

FROST, SNOW AND ICE

Frost and ice on your windows and windscreen can make them opaque, hindering visibility. Ice, tightly packed snow, and rain that freezes as it lands all make roads dangerously slippery: tyres cannot maintain a good grip, and wheels may spin or lock and slide. Braking, steering, and both starting and driving uphill become difficult. Snow may also mask road markings.

Preparing for winter

- Make sure your radiator and windscreen washer bottle contain enough antifreeze.
- If necessary, check the battery.
- Consider fitting tyres designed for use in mud and snow.
- If you expect prolonged snowy weather, fit tyres and wheels with snow chains.
- Put a shovel and sacks in your car.

Preparing to drive in snow and ice

- Before starting a journey, clear frost, ice or snow from the windscreen, windows, mirrors, reflectors and lights. Wiping with a cloth treated with de-icing liquid can help. Warm water clears windows fast, but never use boiling water. Run the engine long enough for the demister and heater to stop ice reforming on the windscreen and rear window. Do not drive until all windows are clear.
- Remove any compacted snow stuck under the car if it might impair braking and steering.
- Use a spade to clear snow in front of your wheels, and lay sacks to give the wheels something to grip.
- Pack a rug and a thermos of hot drink in case you break down.

Setting off in snow and ice

- In cold weather assume wet-looking stretches of road to be icy, and drive with great care.
- If your wheels simply spin when you attempt to drive off, try reversing and then starting forward in a higher than normal gear. On snow, avoid revving the engine. Your wheels will only dig in more deeply.
- Drive off slowly on a slippery surface, but using a higher than normal gear.

Driving along in snow and ice

- On slippery roads drive at a slow speed.
- In snow, use the highest gear possible to prevent the wheels from spinning.
- Only press the controls gently: do not quickly brake, accelerate or turn the steering wheel.
- If it is snowing hard, switch on your windscreen wipers and dipped headlights.
- Leave an extra-long gap between your vehicle and the one ahead.
- Try to turn corners without braking or pressing the clutch pedal. Approach at a low speed in the highest gear possible, and steer steadily around bends.
- Brake extremely gently, especially downhill.
- Engage a low gear to help you reduce speed at the top of a hill.
- Before climbing a hill, use the highest gear that will take you all the way up. Avoid changing halfway up.
- When driving uphill, stay well back from the vehicle ahead so you can keep going if it slows down. (If you are forced to stop halfway up a slippery hill, restarting could prove impossible.)

- Always look out for hazards ahead and prepare to avoid them.
- If you are faced by an oncoming vehicle that is out of control on an icy road, rely on a low gear rather than suddenly braking. Do not try to steer and brake simultaneously.

THE HIGHWAY CODE SAYS:

- Prepare your vehicle for winter. Ensure that the battery is well maintained and that there are appropriate antifreeze agents in the radiator and windscreen washer bottle.
- In freezing or near freezing conditions, drive with great care even if the roads have been gritted. Take care when overtaking vehicles that scatter grit on the road.
- Do not drive in snow unless your journey is essential. If it is, drive slowly but keep in as high a gear as possible to help avoid wheel spin. Avoid sudden acceleration, steering and braking. You MUST use headlights when visibility is seriously reduced by falling snow.
- Watch out for snow ploughs which may throw out snow on either side. Do not overtake them unless the lane you intend to use has been cleared of snow.

STRONG CROSSWINDS

Strong crosswinds – especially on embankments, bridges and motorways – can affect vehicles in potentially dangerous ways, especially when you overtake or are being overtaken. Beware:

- Sudden gusts blowing cyclists and motorcyclists sharply sideways into your path (**a**).
- Cars, including your own, shifting suddenly sideways.

- Being pulled toward a high-sided vehicle as you pass on its lee side, then being pushed away as you receive the full force of the wind (**b**).
- High-sided vehicles toppling over in severe winds on exposed stretches of road.

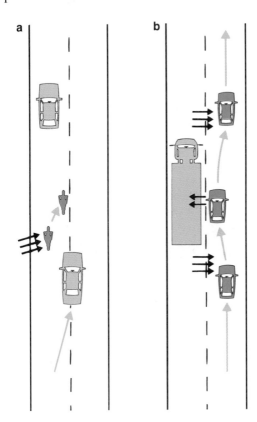

SKIDDING

If its wheels lock, a car may slide or skid, slewing
around out of control and causing an accident.

Why skidding happens

Skidding happens if a driver changes speed or direction
too fast for wheels to maintain their grip. Skids usually
occur on a road made slippery by water, ice, snow, mud
or wet leaves. But skidding can happen on dry roads
too. The main causes of skidding are:

- Braking too sharply.
- Taking corners too sharply.
- Accelerating too sharply.
- Braking as you steer around a sharp bend.

Skid prevention

- Keep brakes and accelerator linkage well maintained
  to prevent skids due to jerky braking or acceleration.
- Look out well ahead for sharp bends and slippery
  road surfaces. Bear in mind that stopping on a
  slippery road may require 10 times the distance
  needed for stopping as on a dry road.
- If the road is slippery, reduce speed by changing
  down rather than braking.
- Treat the clutch pedal and accelerator cautiously.

Getting out of a skid

- Do not touch the brakes.
- Steer into the skid, easing off the accelerator. If your
  vehicle's rear end is sliding left (**a**), steer to the left
  (**b**), then straighten out (**c**). If your vehicle's rear end
  slides to the right, steer to the right.
- Avoid oversteering.

NIGHT DRIVING

Reduced visibility makes seeing and being seen less
easy at night, dusk and dawn than by day.

Using your lights

- Keep lights and reflectors clean and operating well.
- Make sure your headlamps' main and dipped beams
  are properly adjusted.
- Use dipped headlights in poor light (even by day),
  especially if you drive a dark-coloured vehicle.
- If necessary, switch on your lights before the official
  lighting-up time.
- If necessary, leave your lights switched on after
  lighting-up time has ended.
- Use headlamps on all unlit roads, motorways and
  roads bearing fast traffic.
- Switch from dipped to main beam on unlit roads.
- Dip your lights to avoid dazzling oncoming vehicles,
  but first check the position of the left-hand side of the
  road ahead, and look out for hazards.
- Avoid looking at oncoming headlamps. If these
  dazzle you, look to the left kerb, or reduce speed and
  stop if necessary.
- Dip your lights when following another vehicle or if
  one overtakes you. Your light beams should fall on
  the road ahead, not the vehicle (**a**).
- When stopped in traffic or at a junction, engage the
  handbrake. Otherwise your braking lights will stay on
  and might dazzle the driver behind.

Driving and parking at night

- Adjust your speed. Remember that fast driving is less
  safe at night than by day.

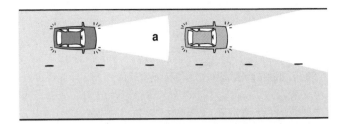

- Set your inside rear-view mirror to its anti-dazzle position.
- Use reflective 'cat's eyes' set in the road to help you judge your road position.
- Look out for illuminated road signs.
- Look out for the lights of cyclists and motorcyclists; they may be less bright and harder to see than those of cars.
- Watch out for pedestrians, cyclists and joggers on poorly lit or shadowy roads.
- Be alert to the distracting effects of illuminated shop signs and wet roads which reflect lights at night.
- Be able to stop within the distance your lights show to be clear.
- Take extra care before overtaking.
- Avoid noisy behaviour like banging doors, revving up and sounding your horn (illegal at night in built-up areas).
- Flash headlamps instead of hooting to warn.
- Switch off headlamps when you stop, even briefly.
- Park your car on the side of the road in the direction of traffic flow (you may park on the right in a one-way street).

- Leave the side lights on unless in a 30 mph speed limit area.
- Avoid parking within 10 m (11 yd) of a junction, or anywhere else where parking is not allowed.

THE HIGHWAY CODE SAYS:

You MUST:

- Make sure all your lights are clean, that they work and that your headlights are properly adjusted – badly adjusted headlights can dazzle other road users and may cause accidents.
- Use side lights between sunset and sunrise.
- Use headlights at night (between half an hour after sunset and half an hour before sunrise) on all roads without street lighting and on roads where the street lights are more than 185 m (202 yd) apart or are not lit.
- Use headlights or front fog lights when visibility is seriously reduced (generally when you cannot see ahead more than 100 m/109 yd).

You should also:

- Use headlights at night on motorways and roads with a speed limit in excess of 50 mph.
- Use dipped headlights at night in built-up areas unless the road is well lit.
- Cut down glare. If your vehicle has dim-dip, use it instead of dipped headlights in dim daytime weather and at night in built-up areas with good street lighting.
- Dip your headlights when meeting vehicles or other road users and to prevent dazzling the driver of a vehicle ahead.
- Slow down or stop if you are dazzled by oncoming headlights.

When parking:
- You must not park at night facing oncoming traffic.
- When parking on the road at night, you MUST leave your side lights on. Cars, goods vehicles not exceeding 1,525 kg (3,362 lb) unladen, invalid carriages and motorcycles, however, may be parked without lights on a road with a speed limit of 30 mph or less if they are:
  - at least 10 m (11 yd) away from any junction, close to the kerb and facing in the direction of the traffic flow; or
  - in a recognized parking place.

BREAKDOWNS

Most breakdowns are due to inadequate maintenance, but even new or well-maintained cars sometimes break down. Go prepared, just in case.

Taking precautions
- Consider joining a national motoring organization that will repair or recover broken-down vehicles.
- Consider carrying a carphone for emergency use.
- Carry a red advance-warning triangle.
- Check that your spare tyre is sound and that your car contains wheel-changing tools.
- Keep a fire extinguisher in your car.
- Keep a first-aid kit in your car.
- Learn first aid.

If you break down
- Brake gently.
- If a puncture makes your car weave from side to side, grasp the steering wheel firmly.

- Steer your car into the side of the road, and stop it off the road if you can. On a motorway, drivers should use the hard shoulder.
- If your car might cause an obstruction or hazard, switch on its hazard warning lights (**a**) and keep sidelights on if visibility is poor.
- Do not open offside doors, especially on motorways.
- Keep passengers and pets well off the road. Make sure they stay on the embankment above or below the vehicle, if it stands on a motorway.
- If you cause an obstruction, set up your advance-warning triangle in the same driving lane as your car, but on the verge or path if the road is narrow. Place it where other road users will see it in time to react (**b**).

Getting help

- Telephone for help unless you can quickly and safely repair the trouble yourself.
- If your car causes an obstruction, warn the police. On motorways, arrows on posts show the nearest emergency telephone. Police control will connect you to a breakdown service.

If you are driving alone and your car breaks down:

- State that you are alone when you telephone for help – especially if you are a woman.
- After telephoning, stay near your vehicle. Get in it (using the front passenger door to avoid traffic) if you feel threatened, and lock the doors once inside.
- Refuse help from strangers; say that help is coming.

Roadside repairs

- Only attempt these if you can do so confidently and without risk of being knocked down by traffic.
- Never change a wheel on a carriageway or motorway hard shoulder or other risky location.

THE HIGHWAY CODE SAYS:

- If you have a breakdown, think first of other traffic. Get your vehicle off the road if possible.
- If your vehicle is causing an obstruction, warn other traffic by using your hazard warning lights. If you carry a red advance-warning triangle, put it on the road at least 50 m (55 yd) before the obstruction and on the same side of the road (150 m/164 yd on the hard shoulder of motorways). At night or in poor visibility, do not stand, or let anyone else stand, behind your vehicle – you could prevent other drivers seeing your rear lights.

ACCIDENTS

If you drive past an accident, do not be distracted from
the road ahead; you might cause another accident. If
you arrive at an accident or were involved but unhurt,
make sure that it does not give rise to another.

After a minor accident

If you are involved in a minor accident in which no one
is injured, follow these procedures:

- Stop.
- Warn other drivers by switching on your hazard
  lights and displaying a red warning triangle.
- Reduce fire risk by switching off your engine and
  stubbing out any cigarettes.
- Exchange names (including the cars' owners'
  names), addresses, car makes and numbers, and car
  insurance details with the other driver.
- Get witnesses' names and addresses.
- List details of the accident: time of day, weather
  conditions, road conditions, vehicle speeds,
  directions, lights, and indicators at the moment of
  impact.
- Photograph the scene if you can.
- Make a sketch map of the scene just before and after
  the accident, including the street names and vehicles
  involved.

In case of fire

If you smell petrol, stop and investigate. If you see
smoke or flames rise from the bonnet:

- Stop as quickly as you can safely pull over.
- Get everyone out of your vehicle.
- Ask someone to phone 999 for help.

- Operate the bonnet release catch but do not lift the bonnet.
- Aim a fire-extinguisher at the narrow gap where the bonnet is open.

After a serious accident

If possible, follow the procedures above, giving priority to preventing another accident and aiding the injured as set out below.

- Make sure someone phones 999 for an ambulance.
- Give what help you can to the injured.
- Move casualties only if they are at risk from explosion, fire or being hit by other vehicles, and do not remove an injured motorcyclist's helmet. Moving someone with a neck injury might leave them permanently paralysed.
- If a vehicle involved had a dangerous load, describe the load's labels when phoning the police or fire brigade and keep well away from the vehicle to avoid breathing noxious fumes.
- If you have not reported to police at the scene, report to police at a station within 24 hours if involved in an accident where someone was injured or where property was damaged and the owner was not found.

First aid – artificial ventilation

To save them from brain damage, unconscious crash victims need oxygen within three minutes if they have stopped breathing.

First, check for breathing:

- Look for regular movements of the chest and abdomen.
- Listen at the victim's mouth.

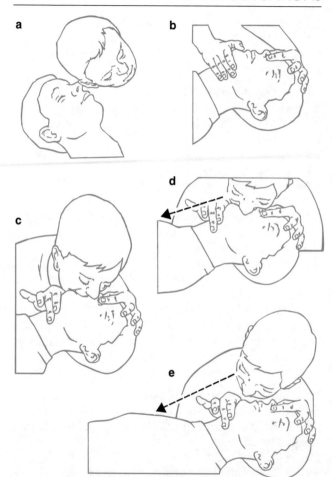

- When you place your face close to the victim's, you should be able to feel his or her breath (**a**).

If the victim is not breathing, give artificial ventilation immediately. The normal procedure is:

- Check the pulse and look and listen for breathing.
- Remove chewing gum, false teeth or other foreign material obstructing the mouth or airway.
- By pushing the chin up with one hand, keep the victim's head tilted far back. Do not do this if you suspect a neck or head injury.
- With your other hand, pinch the victim's nostrils closed (**b**).
- If possible, lay a clean handkerchief – or polythene bag with a slit cut into it – over the victim's mouth. This helps protect against the transmission of HIV.
- Take a deep breath and blow into the victim's mouth (**c**).
- As you breathe, watch out of the corner of your eye to see if the victim's chest rises (**d**).
- Once the chest rises, lift your head and watch for the victim's chest to fall (**e**).
- If you do not see the victim's chest rise when you blow and fall when you stop, there might be an obstruction. Check that the airway is clear.
- Check the pulse again.
- Repeat, giving the first four breaths quickly, until breathing persists unaided.
- If necessary, persist until an ambulance comes.
- With a baby or small child, blow extremely gently, with your mouth covering the victim's mouth and nose.

First aid – shock

If you suspect someone is in shock:

- Have the victim lie down, then keep him or her from moving.
- Raise his or her feet.
- Cover the victim with a blanket or coat.
- Loosen any tight clothing.
- Reassure the victim.
- Check pulse and breathing frequently.

First aid – other procedures

- Treat severe bleeding by pressing firmly on the wound to reduce the local blood flow.
- If a bleeding limb is not broken, keep it raised to reduce the bleeding.
- Do not offer injured people food or drink.
- Keep casualties warm and comfortable.
- Talk quietly but firmly to hysterical people to try to calm them.

THE HIGHWAY CODE SAYS:

- If anything falls from your vehicle on to the road (except a motorway), stop and retrieve it as soon as it is safe to do so. On a motorway, stop at the next emergency telephone to tell the police. Do not try to remove it yourself.
- If you see warning lights or the flashing lights of emergency vehicles, or if vehicles in the distance appear to be moving very slowly or to have stopped, there could have been an accident. Slow down and be ready to stop. Do not be distracted when passing the accident; you could cause another.

- If you are involved in, or stop to give assistance at, an accident:
  - Warn other traffic, e.g. by switching on your hazard warning lights. If possible, get out of your car to ask other stopped drivers to switch off their engines and put out any cigarettes.
  - Arrange for the emergency services to be called immediately with full details of the accident location and any casualties; on a motorway, use the emergency telephone.
  - Do not move injured people unless they are in immediate danger from fire or explosion. Do not remove a motorcyclist's helmet unless it is essential. Be prepared to give first aid.
  - Move uninjured people away from the vehicles to safety.
  - Stay at the scene until the emergency services arrive.
- Vehicles carrying dangerous goods in packages will be marked with plain orange reflective plates.
- Road tankers and vehicles carrying tank containers will have hazard warning plates. If an accident involves a vehicle containing dangerous goods:
  - Switch off engines and DO NOT SMOKE.
  - Keep uninjured people well away from the vehicle and where the wind will not blow dangerous substances toward them.
  - Give the emergency services as much information as possible about the load labels and other markings.

5. The driving test

This chapter broadly follows the sequence of points the examiner will tick off on your Driving Test Report. The test lasts only about 35 minutes. Your instructor may accompany you if you wish.

During the practical part of the test the examiner will give you a series of simple instructions, speaking no more than is necessary, as you drive. After the practical part of the test, the examiner will ask about 10 questions to make sure you know the Highway Code and such things as how to control a skid and the importance of keeping a car well maintained.

Test readiness

Do not apply for a driving test until you can answer 'yes' to all the following questions:
- Have you had plenty of practice?
- Have you covered all the knowledge essential for drivers? (See pp.170–5 for the official syllabus.)
- Can you drive well and confidently at all times?
- Can you do so without your instructor's help?

APPLYING TO TAKE THE TEST

You can apply for your driving test by post, or by telephone if you can pay by Visa or Mastercard credit card. The first step is obtaining Form DL26 from your approved driving instructor (ADI) or nearest Driving Test Centre or from a Driving Standards Agency (DSA) Regional Office. DSA addresses appear at the back of *Your Driving Test*, published by HMSO.

Driving Test Centres and DSA Regional Offices can tell you the fees and hours when testing is done. A higher charge is made for Saturdays and (summer only) evenings where these are available.

Applying by post

1 Obtain form DL26 in plenty of time (expect to wait up to two months or more for your test, depending on your area).
2 Complete Form DL26, giving the test date you would prefer.
3 Post the form to your DSA regional office with the fee, paid by cheque, postal order or credit card.
4 Wait for the DSA regional office to send details of the time, date and place of your test.
5 Get in touch with your DSA regional office if you have not received these details within two weeks.

Applying by telephone

You need a valid Visa or Mastercard credit card in your name.

1 Complete Form DL26.
2 From Form DL26 find the credit card 'hotline' telephone number for your area.
3 With your completed form and credit card handy, telephone the credit card 'hotline'.
4 You must be able to tell the driving test booking clerk the following information:
- Driver number (on your provisional licence).
- Personal details.
- Disability details, if any (e.g. affecting your movement or hearing).
- Driving school code number (if you know it).

- Desired date.
- Unavailable dates.
- Whether you could perform a test at short notice.

The booking clerk will tell you your appointment date, and you will receive confirmation in the post.

If you have to postpone or cancel, tell your DSA regional office at least 10 working days before the test date. If you give shorter notice you forfeit your fee.

ESSENTIAL KNOWLEDGE

In order to pass the driving test you must achieve a level of competence as set out below. This is based on the recommended syllabus published in HMSO's *Your Driving Test*.

You must have:

- A thorough knowledge of the Highway Code and motoring laws.
- A thorough understanding of your responsibilities as a driver.

Legal requirements

To learn to drive you must:

- Be at least 17 years old, or 16 if you receive a mobility allowance for a disability.
- Be able to read in good daylight (with glasses or contact lenses if necessary) a motor vehicle numberplate 20.5 m (approx. 67 ft) away with letters 79.4 mm (3.1 in.) high.
- Be medically fit to drive.
- Hold a provisional licence or comply with the conditions for holding a provisional licence.
- Ensure that your vehicle:
  - Is legally roadworthy.
  - Has a current test certificate, if over prescribed age.

- Is properly licensed with correct tax disc displayed.
- Make sure your vehicle is properly insured for the test.
- Display L-plates visible from the front and back of the vehicle.
- Be supervised by a person who:
  - Has held a full UK licence for at least three years for the kind of vehicle being used.
  - Is at least 21 years old.
- Wear a seat belt, unless granted exemption, and see that all the seat belts in the vehicle are free from defects.
- Ensure that children under 14 are suitably restrained.
- Be aware of the legal requirement to declare medical conditions which could affect safe driving. If a vehicle has been adapted for disability, ensure that the adaptations are suitable to control the vehicle safely.
- Know the rules on the issue, presentation or display of:
  - Driving licences.
  - Insurance certificates.
  - Tax discs.

Car controls, equipment and components
You must:
- Understand the function of, and use competently the following controls:
  - accelerator
  - clutch
  - gears
  - foot brake
  - handbrake
  - steering
- Know the function of other controls and switches in the car that have a bearing on road safety and use them competently.
- Understand the meaning of the gauges and other displays on the instrument panel.
- Know the legal requirements for the vehicle.

- Be able to carry out routine checks – e.g. tyre pressure and oil level – and identify defects especially with:
  - steering
  - brakes
  - tyres
  - seat belts
  - lights
  - reflectors
  - direction indicators
  - wipers and washers
  - horn
  - rear-view mirrors
  - speedometer
  - exhaust system
- Know the safety factors related to vehicle loading.

Road user behaviour
You must:
- Know the most common causes of accidents.
- Know which road users are most at risk and how to reduce that risk.
- Know the rules, risks and effects of drinking and driving.
- Know the effect of fatigue, illness and drugs on driving performance.
- Be aware of age-dependent problems among road users, especially children, teenagers and the elderly.
- Be alert and able to anticipate the likely actions of other road users and to suggest appropriate precautions.
- Be aware that courtesy and consideration towards road users are essential for safe driving.

Vehicle characteristics
You must:
- Know the most important principles concerning braking distances and road holding under various road and weather conditions.
- Know the handling characteristics of other vehicles with regard to stability, speed, braking and manoeuvrability.
- Know that some vehicles are less easily seen than others.
- Be able to assess the risks caused by characteristics of

other vehicles and suggest precautions that can be taken, for example:

- Large commercial vehicles pulling to the right before turning left.
- Blind spots for drivers of some commercial vehicles.
- Bicycles and motorcycles being buffeted by strong wind.

Road and weather conditions

You must:

- Know the particular hazards of driving in both daylight and the dark.
- Know the particular hazards of driving on different types of road, for example on single carriageways, including country lanes, on three-lane roads and on dual-carriageways and motorways.
- Gain experience in driving on urban and higher-speed roads (but not motorways) in both daylight and darkness.
- Know which road surfaces provide better or poorer grip when braking.
- Know the hazards caused by bad weather, for example:
  - rain
  - snow
  - strong crosswinds
  - fog
  - icy roads
- Be able to assess the risks caused by road and traffic conditions, be aware of how the conditions may cause others to drive unsafely, and be able to take appropriate precautions.

Traffic signs, rules and regulations

You must:

- Have a sound knowledge of the meaning of traffic signs and road markings, for example:
  - speed limits

- parking restrictions
- zebra and pelican crossings

Car control and road procedure

You must have the knowledge and skill to carry out the following tasks, in both daylight and darkness, safely and competently, making proper use of mirrors, observation and signals:

- Take necessary precautions before getting into or out of the vehicle.
- Before starting the engine:
  - Carry out the safety checks, including fastening the seat belts (see pp.178—9).
  - Take proper precautions.
- Start the engine and move off:
  - Straight ahead and at an angle.
  - On the level, uphill and downhill.
- Select the correct road position for norrnal driving.
- Make proper observations in all traffic conditions.
- Drive at a speed suitable for road and traffic conditions.
- React promptly to all risks.
- Change traffic lanes.
- Pass stationary vehicles.
- Meet, overtake and cross the path of other vehicles.
- Turn right and left, and at junctions, including crossroads and roundabouts.
- Drive ahead at crossroads and roundabouts.
- Keep a safe distance behind vehicles ahead.
- Act correctly at pedestrian crossings.
- Show proper regard for the safety of other road users, with particular care towards the most vulnerable.
- Drive on both urban and rural roads and, where possible, dual carriageways – keeping up with the traffic flow where it is safe and proper to do so.

- Comply with traffic regulations and traffic signs and signals given by the police, traffic wardens and other road users.
- Stop the vehicle safely, normally and in an emergency, without locking the wheels.
- Turn the vehicle in the road to face the opposite way using the forward and reverse gears.
- Reverse the vehicle into a side turning, keeping reasonably close to the kerb.
- Park parallel to the kerb while driving in reverse gear. Park the vehicle in a multi-storey car park, or other parking bay, on the level, uphill and downhill, both in forward and reverse direction.
- Cross all types of railway level crossings.

Additional knowledge

You must know:

- The importance of correct tyre pressures.
- How to avoid and correct skids.
- How to drive through floods and flooded areas.
- What to do if involved in an accident or breakdown, including the special arrangements for accidents and breakdowns on motorways.
- Basic first aid for use on the road as set out in the Highway Code.
- How to deter car thieves.

Motorway driving

You must gain a sound knowledge of the special rules, regulations and driving techniques for motorway driving before taking your test. After passing your test, you should take motorway lessons with an ADI before driving unsupervised on motorways.

BEFORE YOUR TEST

Before setting off to the test centre, tick off all items
from the following checklist, taking with you any
documents the examiner might ask to see.

Vehicle checklist

- If you take the test using a car with automatic
  transmission, you will be qualified to drive only
  automatic cars. Taking the test on a car with manual
  gears qualifies you to drive either type.
- Your vehicle must meet certain requirements for a car
  driving test, e.g. weigh under 7.5 tonnes.
- It must be mechanically sound.
- Its tyres must be fully inflated and sound.
- All controls, lights, indicators, washers and wipers,
  etc. must work properly.
- Windows and mirrors must be clean.
- The vehicle must give a clear view through the rear
  window when driver and examiner look back.
- If over the prescribed age, it must have an MOT
  certificate.
- It must be insured for its current use and for you as a
  driver.
- It must be licensed and properly display a current tax
  disc.
- It must display secure L-plates in front and rear.
- It should have plenty of fuel for the test.

Personal checklist

- Revise the Highway Code.
- Find out where the test centre is.
- Allow time to get there with your instructor.
- Take the notification of appointment sent to you by

your DSA regional office.

- Take your provisional driving licence signed by you, or other proof of identity, e.g. a signed passport.
- Take your car's insurance certificate (which must be valid for your driving test) and MOT certificate if the car needs one.
- Take glasses if you need them for driving.

Note: Do not at any point offer the examiner a bribe. This is a criminal offence.

EYESIGHT TEST

Test requirement

- You must be able to read a vehicle numberplate with letters 79.4 mm (3.1 in.) high in good daylight from a distance of 20.5 m (67 ft). Wear glasses or contact lenses if you need them and always use them for driving.

Test procedure

- The examiner will show you a vehicle and ask you to read its numberplate. If you cannot, the examiner will repeat the test after first measuring the distance. If you fail the eyesight test you have failed the driving test.

HIGHWAY CODE
Test requirements
During the test, you must show that you understand the
Highway Code and obey the rules it lays down.

After the test, you must answer the examiner's
questions about the Highway Code and some important
items that it does not include, such as:

- The meanings of some traffic signs.
- Car and road safety.
- How poor weather affects the way vehicles handle
  and behave.
- The condition of tyres.

In future, candidates may also be required to know
basic vehicle maintenance.

Test procedure
- Show that you obey the Highway Code during the
  practical part of your test.
- Answer the examiner's questions correctly after the
  test. Minor errors will not necessarily make you fail.

BEFORE STARTING THE ENGINE
Test requirements
You must make sure that:

- Doors are fully shut (**a**).
- Seat and headrest are adjusted (**b**).
- Seat belt is fastened (**c**).
- Driving mirrors are adjusted (**d**).
- Handbrake is on (**e**).
- Gear level is in neutral (**f**).

You must avoid:

- Closing a door while driving.

- Adjusting your seat while driving.
- Fastening your seat belt while driving.
- Adjusting a mirror while driving.
- Applying the gear lever or handbrake longer than you need to.

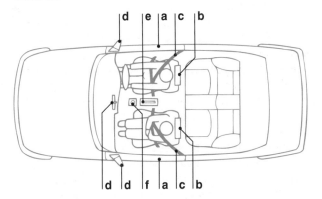

HANDLING AND UNDERSTANDING CONTROLS

Test requirements

You must use the car controls smoothly, correctly, safely and at the right time. There is no specific test exercise, but the examiner will watch to see that you understand and use car controls properly throughout the test.

Tested skills

Handbrake Release it to drive off. Apply it when stopped for more than a moment or two. Never apply it while the car is still moving.

Accelerator Press this down as you release the clutch pedal to obtain a smooth start. Then accelerate smoothly away. Avoid sudden acceleration.

Clutch Gradually release the clutch pedal as you gradually press the accelerator for a smooth start. Avoid jerky clutch pedal movements as you drive away or change gear. Press the clutch just before stopping. Never 'freewheel' (or 'coast') with the clutch pedal pressed down.

Gears Change gear to suit your speed and the traffic. Change gear in time to anticipate any problem or hazard ahead. Avoid looking down at the gear lever or grasping it longer than necessary. Never 'freewheel' in neutral.

Steering Hold the wheel with your hands at the 'ten-to-two' or 'quarter-to-three' position. Do not use the door as an arm rest. Steer smoothly, letting the wheel slide up through the fingers of one hand, while the other is pulling it down. Do not cross one hand over the other. Steer round a corner by turning the wheel just before getting there. Avoid turning too soon or too late; you might cut a corner, hit a kerb, or swing into the wrong traffic lane. After completing a turn, straighten the wheel. Do not leave it to spin back on its own.

Foot brake Brake in good time, and no more than necessary. Avoid braking hard at the last moment except in an emergency.

Various controls and switches You must be able to show that you know the purpose of switches or other controls affecting your vehicle's safety. You must be able to identify the various gauges and warning lights on the instrument panel.

MOVING OFF

Test requirements

The examiner will expect you to show you can move off safely with your vehicle under control: on level ground, from behind a parked car, and perhaps on a hill.

Test procedure

- Use mirrors, and signal if appropriate.
- Look around for traffic and pedestrians possibly hidden from your mirrors. Do not drive off without looking, or so as to make other road users stop or swerve round you. Be aware that when moving off from behind a parked car (**a**), your front end might extend into the path of oncoming traffic, so check in all directions.
- Straighten out as soon as you can (**b**), and drive off with safe and controlled use of the accelerator, clutch, brakes and steering. Avoid poor coordination of controls, especially where this causes the engine to stall. Use the appropriate gear.

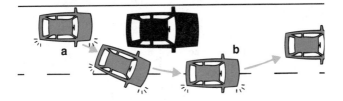

●As soon as you are able, position yourself in your lane.

EMERGENCY STOP
Test requirements
You must be able to stop the car as quickly as possible, but under control, without skidding or veering off course and without danger to other road users.

Test procedure
●The examiner asks you to stop at the side of the road.
●The examiner asks you to make an emergency stop when he or she gives you the signal, and demonstrates the signal by raising his or her arm.
●Apply the handbrake, put the car into first gear, and check all around the car to be sure it is safe to drive off. If it is, do so.
●The examiner signals and you stop as quickly as it is safely possible, pressing the foot brake and clutch pedals down firmly and fast, without stamping. Beware skidding, especially if the road is wet after rain. If the road is wet, pump the brake pedal.

REVERSING INTO A LIMITED OPENING
Test requirement
You must be able to reverse around a corner in the correct manner, safely, smoothly and in control of your vehicle. You may be asked to reverse into an opening on the left or the right. (Drivers of vans without side windows might be asked to reverse into an opening on the right.)

Test procedure

- The examiner asks you to stop on the left just after a side road off to the left (**a**).
- The examiner shows you the side road and asks you to reverse into it.
- You may unfasten your seat belt for this test if necessary.
- Check your mirrors and look around until it is safe to proceed.
- Reverse slowly around the corner, watching for vehicles and pedestrians. Keep fairly close to the kerb (**b**), but avoid hitting it or swinging out. You might have to stop to let vehicles (**c**) or pedestrians pass.

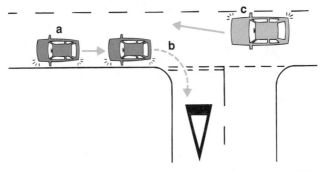

- Straighten out and continue reversing for a reasonable distance (**d** overleaf), so that you are clear of the main road (**e** overleaf).

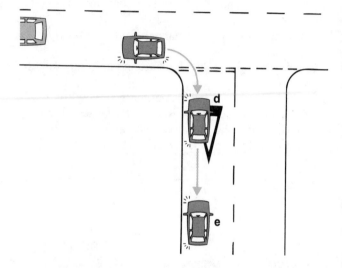

● If you had unfastened your seat belt, refasten it when
the test is complete and before moving off.

REVERSE PARKING
Test requirement
You must be able to reverse into a space about as long
as two cars in order to park safely by the kerb.

Test procedure
● The examiner indicates a parked car (**a**) and asks you
to reverse to park behind it.

- Stop beside the parked car so both bonnets are level (**b**). You should be far enough out to reverse safely. Avoid stopping too close to the parked car.
- Engage reverse gear.
- Look all around until it is safe to proceed.
- Reverse slowly and steadily into the space behind the parked car, in a single manoeuvre (**c**). Beware the parked car's offside rear wing. Avoid unnecessary swinging about. Watch all the time for vehicles and pedestrians, and be considerate of them.
- Stop parallel and close to the kerb within the space of two car lengths behind the parked car (**d**). Avoid mounting the kerb, and avoid parking too far out.

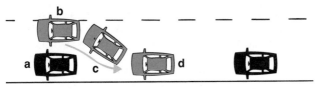

TURNING IN THE ROAD
Test requirement
You must be able to use forward and reverse gears to turn your vehicle in a road until it faces the opposite way, and achieve this in only three moves if possible. You must show proper use of the controls to move and stop smoothly. You must show consideration to other road users and not put them in danger.

Test procedure
- The examiner indicates a suitable stretch of road and asks you to stop on the left (**a**).
- The examiner asks you to turn your vehicle around.
- Check that the road is clear in both directions.
- Drive forward slowly in first gear, turning the steering wheel hard to the right.
- Turn the steering wheel left just before stopping short of the opposite kerb (**b**).
- Make visual checks all around.
- When it is safe to do so, reverse slowly across the road, turning the steering wheel hard to the left.
- Turn the steering wheel right just before stopping short of the kerb behind you (**c**).
- If necessary, drive forward and back again to complete your turn.
- When you can safely do so, drive forward to straighten up on the left-hand side of the road (**d**). You are now facing the opposite way to the direction you started in.

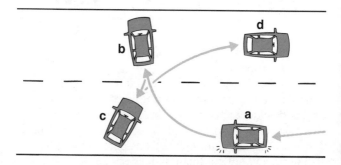

USING MIRRORS AND LOOKING BACK

Test requirements

You must correctly use mirrors to assess the situation behind you, especially before signalling or changing speed or direction. When necessary, reinforce this with a quick backward glance. There is no specific test procedure, but throughout the test the examiner notices if you look in your mirrors, especially when:

- starting to drive
- accelerating
- signalling
- changing direction
- changing lanes
- overtaking
- turning left or right
- slowing or stopping
- opening your door

Tested skills

- Always look in your mirrors before signalling.
- Always look and signal before making a manoeuvre.
- Remember that mirrors cannot reveal everything behind or almost alongside you. When necessary, take a quick backward glance to check that the area in your blind spot is clear.
- Act on what you see. React sensibly and with consideration for other road users.

SIGNALLING

Test requirements

You must signal well ahead to let other road users and pedestrians know your intentions and to give them time to respond safely. There is no specific test procedure, but the examiner notices whether, when and how you signal throughout the test.

Tested skills

- Give signals in good time.
- Only use those signals in the Highway Code.
- Make sure your signals are appropriate.
- When necessary, use a hand signal described in the Highway Code (see opposite). Make sure you give it clearly.
- Do not wave pedestrians across a road.
- Cancel each signal after it is no longer needed.

RESPONDING TO SIGNS AND SIGNALS

Test requirements

You must show that you understand and respond to traffic signs and the signals of other drivers. The examiner will be looking specifically at your ability to do the following.

Tested skills

- Follow the road ahead unless traffic signs indicate or the examiner tells you otherwise.
- Understand and respond to traffic signs sufficiently early.
- Understand and respond to road markings sufficiently early.
- Behave correctly at traffic lights. This includes making sure your way is clear before driving on, even when the lights are green.
- Respond to signals by other road users.

Highway code hand signals

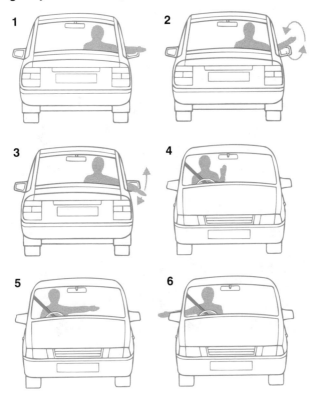

1 I intend moving to the right or turning right.
2 I intend moving to the left or turning left.
3 I intend slowing down or stopping.
4 I intend driving straight on.
5 I intend turning left.
6 I intend turning right.

- Obey the signals of police officers, traffic wardens and school crossing patrols.
- Reduce speed on roads with traffic calming devices: humps, 20 mph speed limit signs, or paving, bollards or posts which make a road narrow.

Sample traffic signs

20 mph maximum

No vehicles

Give priority to vehicles from opposite direction

Distance over which road humps extend

Road narrows at right

Roadworks

MAKING PROGRESS AT A SAFE SPEED
Test requirements

You must drive along at a steady, reasonable speed. There is no specific test exercise, but throughout the test the examiner notices how well and confidently you keep up with the flow of traffic, how safely you adjust your speed to the driving conditions, and how promptly you move off at junctions when you can go ahead safely.

Tested skills

- Maintain a steady speed except when you overtake or have to slow down. Do not keep speeding up and slowing down.
- Avoid driving slowly enough to delay the traffic behind you if the road ahead is clear (**a**).
- Avoid slowing down more than you need to when you see a junction or other hazard ahead.
- Avoid waiting at junctions longer than necessary.
- Drive within the speed limit.
- Avoid driving too fast for the conditions, even if within the speed limit.
- Adjust your speed according to:
  - speed limit
  - road type and surface
  - road signs

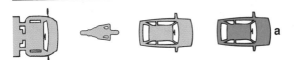

- traffic density and speed
- weather and visibility
- Be certain you can safely stop within the space ahead that you can see to be clear.
- Leave a safe gap between your vehicle and others.
- Extend this gap on a wet or slippery road.

COPING WITH A HAZARD

Test requirements

You must show that you can anticipate hazards (anything making you alter your speed or direction), then follow the correct sequence of actions. Hazards include junctions and roundabouts as well as other road users, such as cyclists and pedestrians. Your examiner will notice how you respond to hazards throughout the test, paying special attention to your use of the mirror/signal/manoeuvre sequence, vehicle positioning and speed, and alertness and judgement.

Test procedure

- Notice a hazard when it is still well ahead.
- Look in your mirrors to check following vehicles.
- Signal well ahead that you will slow down or change direction.
- When it is safe, complete your manoeuvre.

Procedures for specific hazards follow.

ROAD JUNCTIONS AND ROUNDABOUTS

Test requirements

You must show that you use the mirror/signal/ manoeuvre sequence when approaching a junction or roundabout, that you slow down properly after

determining the best approach speed and position, and
that you follow road signs and observe other traffic.
There is no specific test exercise.

Tested skills
- Look in your mirrors.
- Signal.
- Reduce speed as you approach the hazard.
- If turning left from a road without lane markings,
  keep left. Beware pedestrians crossing your path or
  cyclists (**a**) or motorcyclists moving up on your
  inside.

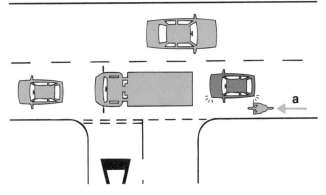

- If turning right from a road without lane markings,
  move near the centre of the road.
- If your approach road has several lanes, get into the
  appropriate lane.
- Note and obey junction road signs and markings.
- Slow down at the junction or roundabout, if necessary
  stopping without sudden braking.

- Look in all directions before entering the junction or roundabout.
- Wait for a sufficient break in the traffic.
- Enter the junction or roundabout as soon as it is safe.
- Take special care not to cut right-hand corners.

OVERTAKING

Test requirements

You must show that you overtake only when it is safe to do so, using the mirror/signal/manoeuvre sequence, observing the speed limit, and leaving enough space for whatever you overtake. There is no specific exercise.

Tested skills

- Do not overtake if you cannot see your way clear ahead, the road is narrow, road signs or markings forbid overtaking, you are about to be overtaken, or you cannot overtake quickly and safely.
- Wait until you have a clear view of the road ahead.
- Assess the positions and speeds of oncoming vehicles and those ahead and behind. Be sure to make use of your mirrors.
- When it is safe, signal and overtake. You must not exceed the speed limit or make other vehicles change speed or course.
- Leave enough space for the vehicle you are overtaking. Allow horse riders, cyclists (**a**) and motorcyclists as much room as a car.
- After overtaking, return to your original lane without moving in too quickly ahead of the vehicle you overtook ('cutting in').
- Cancel your signal.

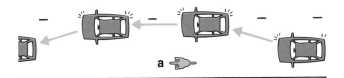

ONCOMING AND STATIONARY VEHICLES

Test requirements

You must safely and confidently pass stationary vehicles and cope with oncoming traffic, especially on narrow roads or roads with parked cars or other obstructions. There is no specific test exercise.

Tested skills

- Try to leave at least a car door's width between stationary vehicles and your car as you pass (**a**).
- Be alert for pedestrians stepping out between parked vehicles, or vehicle doors opening, or stationary vehicles moving off unexpectedly.

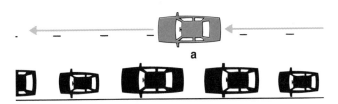

- Remember to use the mirror/signal/manoeuvre
  sequence if you need to slow down or stop.

Meeting oncoming vehicles requires special skill and
judgement on narrow roads or roads with obstructions
such as parked cars – places where two vehicles cannot
pass safely. If you approach an obstruction on your side
of the road and see an oncoming vehicle:

- Use the mirror/signal/manoeuvre sequence.
- Slow down, ready to stop.
- Give way to the oncoming vehicle (**a**).
- If you must stop, do so far enough before the
  obstruction to see the road beyond, and leave room to
  pull out and pass when it is safe (**b**).
- Do not cause the oncoming vehicle to slow down,
  swerve to avoid you, or stop.
- When the oncoming vehicle has passed, check your
  mirrors, signal, and move off when it is safe.
- Act decisively when you stop and drive off.

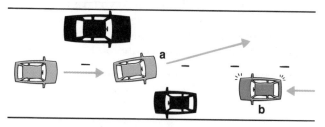

CROSSING ANOTHER VEHICLE'S PATH
Test requirement
You must be able to cross the path of oncoming cars
safely and confidently, as when turning right into a
driveway or at a junction. There is no specific exercise.

Tested skills

- As you approach your turning point, use the mirror/signal/manoeuvre sequence (**a**).
- Get as near the centre of the road as you safely can.
- Look ahead for oncoming traffic.
- Slow down as you reach your turning point (**b**), and stop if you cannot safely proceed. Avoid overshooting or undershooting your turning point.
- Do not turn yet if this would make other vehicles swerve, reduce speed, or stop.
- Look all around. Beware pedestrians who might be about to cross your path.
- Turn correctly when it is safe to proceed (**c**). Avoid cutting the corner.

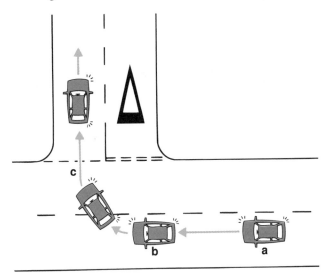

POSITIONING IN TRAFFIC

Test requirements

You must maintain a safe speed when following
another vehicle. Drive at a speed that allows you to
stop safely in the space ahead which you can see to be
clear. There is no specific test exercise.

Tested skills

- Judge the gap between your vehicle and the one in
  front.
- Keep a safe stopping distance behind the vehicle in
  front. At normal speed on dry roads allow a two-
  second gap (**a**). Double this if road or weather
  conditions are poor (**b**).
- Frequently check your mirrors.
- Watch out ahead for brake lights, direction indicators,
  traffic lights, or other hints that the vehicle in front
  might slow down or stop.

Dry weather – dry road condition

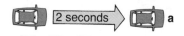

Wet weather - poor road condition

- Allow space and time to use the mirror/signal/
manoeuvre sequence in case you have to slow down
or stop behind the vehicle ahead. Avoid having to
swerve or brake suddenly.

EXERCISING LANE DISCIPLINE

Test requirements

You must drive on the left-hand side of the road when
possible. Steer a steady course past parked vehicles.
Obey lane markings, especially in one-way streets, at
junctions and roundabouts, and bus lanes (avoiding
these when in use). Change lanes in good time after
using the mirror/signal/manoeuvre sequence. There is
no specific test exercise.

Tested skills

- Keep well to the left when you can.
- Avoid driving close to the middle of the road.
- Avoid driving too near the kerb.
- Steer clear of parked vehicles.
- Do not weave in and out of parked vehicles.
- Look well ahead for junctions and lane markings,
especially arrows on the road.
- Obey these lane markings.
- Use the mirror/signal/manoeuvre sequence if you
need to change lanes.
- Move into the correct lane or (if none is marked) the
correct left or right road position. Do this in good
time, not at the last moment.
- Do not straddle lanes or shift lanes for no reason.
- Do not position your vehicle in a way that obstructs
others, especially at a junction or roundabout.

PEDESTRIAN CROSSINGS

Test requirement

You must show pedestrians consideration and courtesy by slowing or stopping for them at pedestrian crossings. There is no specific test exercise.

Tested skills

- Look out well ahead for pedestrian crossings.
- Approach crossings slowly enough to stop if you have to.
- Check your mirrors and if necessary give the correct slowing-down arm signal.
- Never overtake between the zig-zag road markings just before and after a pedestrian crossing.
- Avoid stopping on a crossing.
- Stop for anyone waiting to cross or crossing a zebra crossing (**a**).

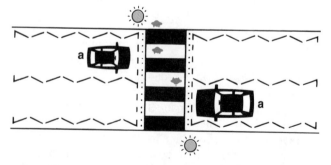

- Stop if a pelican crossing's lights are red.
- Give way to pedestrians on a pelican crossing when its amber lights are flashing (**b**).

- Do not wave pedestrians across a crossing.
- Do not hurry pedestrians along by, for example, inching forward, revving up, or hooting.
- When it is safe, drive on but keep watching for danger.

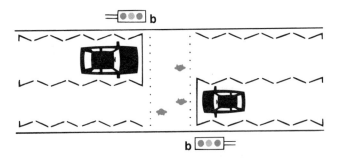

SELECTING A SAFE STOPPING PLACE

Test requirement

You must choose somewhere to stop close to the side of the road where your vehicle does not cause a hazard or an obstruction (see examples on p.91). There is no specific test exercise.

Tested skills

- Look ahead for a place where you can pull in without hindering or endangering other road users. Avoid stopping where signs or road markings forbid it.
- When you see a suitable place, check your mirror, signal, and pull in. Avoid stopping without giving other road users adequate warning.

- Stop with your car near and parallel to the edge of the road, without mounting the kerb (**a**).

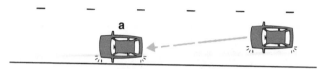

SHOWING AWARENESS AND ANTICIPATION

Test requirements

You must show awareness of all other road users all the time. Anticipate other road users' behaviour which might give rise to danger, and respond promptly with consideration for safety. There is no specific test for these items, but as you drive use the following procedures.

- Watch out for cyclists and motorcyclists riding up on your left at junctions or in slow traffic.
- Watch out for child cyclists, and all cyclists if you cross a cycle lane (**a** opposite) or a bus lane.
- When you turn from one road into another, give way to pedestrians crossing in front of you.
- Watch out for unexpected pedestrian behaviour, giving extra consideration to the old, young, infirm and disabled.
- Be considerate to horse riders, herders and others in charge of animals.

- Avoid showing impatience with pedestrians, cyclists and other road users.
- Plan ahead to avoid making last-minute reactions to hazards.

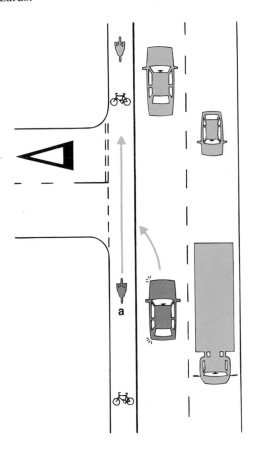

QUESTIONS

The driving test usually ends with a few questions to test your knowledge of the Highway Code and other motoring matters, including vehicle safety and motorway driving (see pp.126-9). The examiner will also expect you to know about making routine car safety checks and to understand such things as how extra passengers or a loaded roof rack can affect the way your car handles.

Here are a few of the scores of questions that the examiner might ask.

1 What should a driver do before opening his or her door?

2 What do the three main shapes of road signs mean?

3 What are the three kinds of white line in the middle of a road and what do they mean?

4 What should you do before changing course?

5 At what speed should you always drive?

6 What should you do if a traffic light turns amber as you approach?

7 What does the Highway Code say about parking and traffic signs?

8 How fast may you drive in a built-up area?

9 What does the Highway Code say about leaving or entering a roadside property?

10 What should you do if involved in an accident involving injury to someone else or damage to someone's property?

11 Which lane should you drive in on a motorway?

Answers

1 Look around to check that no one, especially a cyclist or pedestrian, will hit the door.

2 Circular signs give an order. Triangular signs give a warning. Rectangular signs give information.

3 Short, long, and unbroken. Short lines indicate lane boundaries. Longer lines indicate a hazard. Where there are double white lines you may not cross a continuous line on your side of the road unless safely passing a stationary obstruction or entering or leaving a side road.

4 Check your mirrors and signal before making your manoeuvre.

5 The speed at which you can safely stop within the distance you can see to be clear ahead, and within the speed limit.

6 Stop unless you have crossed the line or are so near it that stopping might cause an accident.

7 Do not park where your vehicle obscures a traffic sign, including one painted on the carriageway.

8 You may drive up to 30 mph where there are street lights except where small signs show a higher speed.

9 Give way to passing road traffic and to pedestrians walking along the pavement.

10 Stop. Unless injured, act to prevent further accidents. If necessary, begin first aid quickly and call, or have someone else call, for help. Get and give information as laid down in the Highway Code. Report the accident to the police within 24 hours if they are not at the scene.

11 You should drive in the left-hand lane unless you are overtaking or that lane is slower than you are.

6. After the test

IF YOU FAILED

The examiner will hand you a statement sheet marked with the main reasons why you failed. The examiner will not discuss these in detail, although an oral explanation may be offered.

Why you failed

These are the 10 most common reasons for failing a driving test, in order of frequency.

1 Failing to steer correctly, as in:
- Taking both hands off the wheel.
- Steering an unsteady course.
- Steering into a corner too early or too late.

2 Failing to use the gears properly, as in:
- Staying in low gear throughout.
- Looking down at the gear lever.
- Coasting in neutral.

3 Failing to move off safely and under control, as in:
- Pulling out without making full safety checks.
- Pulling out without signalling.
- Rolling back on a hill.

4 Failing to judge speed correctly, as in:
- Driving too fast for the road conditions.
- Driving too slowly to keep up with the traffic.
- Waiting at junctions where it is safe to proceed.

5 Failing to use mirrors correctly, as in:
- Not using side mirrors.
- Failing to check mirrors before turning.

- Checking mirrors before turning but failing to signal to following vehicles first.

6 Failing to signal and act on traffic signs, as in:

- Forgetting to signal a left or right turn.
- Signalling a turn too late to warn following vehicles.
- Forgetting to switch off an indicator.

7 Failing to approach crossroads and junctions at the correct speed and with proper observation, as in:

- Approaching a junction too fast.
- Approaching a junction too slowly and holding up traffic.
- Turning left across a cyclist's path.
- Approaching a junction in the wrong traffic lane.
- Stopping at a junction too soon to be able to see when each way is clear.

8 Failing to negotiate left and right turns properly, as in:

- Swinging wide on a left turn.
- Cutting a corner when turning right.
- Failing to take account of other traffic.

9 Failing to negotiate roundabouts and exercise lane discipline, as in:

- Approaching a roundabout in the wrong traffic lane for your intended exit.
- Changing lanes without taking other traffic into account.

10 Failing to reverse and turn in the road correctly, as in:

- Failing to look out for children and vehicles.
- Losing clutch control.
- Steering too late or too soon.
- Mounting the kerb.

Other common reasons for failure
- Failing the eyesight test.
- Not stopping at a STOP sign, or not giving way at a GIVE WAY sign or pedestrian crossing.
- Driving through a red traffic light.
- Exceeding a speed limit.
- Not showing awareness of other road users.
- Not showing consideration to other road users.
- Driving too near cyclists or parked vehicles when overtaking.
- Not completing an emergency stop fast enough and under control.
- Not keeping well to the left except when changing lanes to overtake or turn right.
- Poor use of brakes, clutch, gears or steering.
- Poor road positioning.
- Being unable to answer most of the examiner's simple Highway Code questions.
- Causing an accident.
- Showing such poor control of your car that the examiner stops the test on the spot and forbids you to drive on without an instructor.

If you have failed, prepare to retake the test by practising on the road (with your driving instructor) as much as possible, and by revising the Highway Code. You must wait one month before retaking the test.

Appeals
If you believe you failed because your test was not carried out properly, you may appeal within six months (21 days in Scotland).

IF YOU PASSED

- Take out a full driving licence (see pp.210–11).
- Remove your L-plates.
- You may now drive on motorways.

Be aware of the law and your responsibilities as a driver:

- Be sure the vehicle you drive stays roadworthy.
- Be sure it has a valid MOT certificate if one is needed on account of the car's age (see pp.214–15).
- Be sure your car is insured (see pp.212–13), has a valid vehicle excise licence and displays its tax disc inside the bottom left-hand side of the windscreen.
- Produce your driving licence, insurance certificate, tax disc, and (if appropriate) MOT certificate if the police ask to see them with good reason.
- Do not overload your vehicle.
- Do not carry loads that stick out dangerously, obscure numberplates, or are not secured properly.
- Know your responsibility as a driver for the safety of children in your vehicle (see pp.124–25).
- Do not drink and drive and do not drive under the influence of drugs or medicines.
- Be sure you are medically fit to drive. Notify the authorities of any medical condition that might affect safe driving.
- If your car is modified for a disability make sure you can still safely control the vehicle.
- Do not drive if you feel tired or ill.
- On a long drive let in plenty of fresh air and stop if you feel sleepy.
- Do not use a hand-held telephone or microphone while you drive or speak into a hands-free microphone if it affects driving concentration.

READING YOUR LICENCE

1 Title of licence.
2 Period for which licence is valid.
3 Driver number.
4 Driver's personal details and signature.

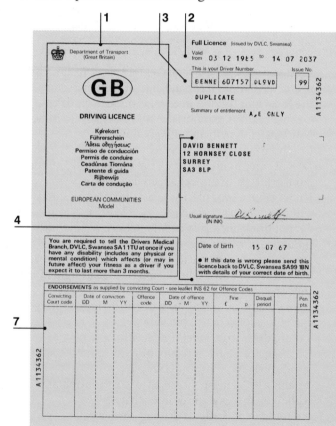

5 Types of vehicles licence holder is entitled to drive.
6 Types of vehicles licence holder may drive only as a learner under instruction.
7 Endorsements: details of licence holder's driving offences, if any.

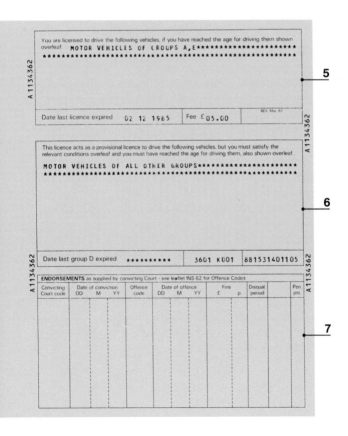

ARRANGING INSURANCE

It is illegal to drive without insurance, and also dangerous. If you are involved in an accident causing injury or property damage and you are driving uninsured, you could be prosecuted. If you have just received your licence and will be taking on responsibility for a car for the first time, arrange for appropriate insurance cover immediately.

Types and costs

There are three main types of cover:

- **Third party** (cheapest). This does not cover you against injury or your car against damage or theft.
- **Third party, fire and theft** (next cheapest). This does not cover you against injury or your car against anything except theft and fire damage.
- **Comprehensive** (most expensive). This covers you against injury and your vehicle against theft, fire and other damage.

In addition, costs depend on a number of factors:

- Your age.
- Where you live.
- How you intend to use the car (e.g. regular trips to work, long journeys).
- Your car's make and the power of its engine.
- Any prior court convictions.

Find out what the 'excess' is for your policy. This is the amount you're expected to pay on any claim – usually £50 or £100.

Once you have taken out insurance cover, you will receive a certificate of insurance – which you must produce if involved in an accident and to renew your vehicle excise licence – and a policy document outlining the terms of your contract. Keep both documents in a safe place.

VEHICLE SECURITY

In the United Kingdom alone, thieves steal or break into a car every few seconds. Car thefts are costly and inconvenient but often avoidable. Do your best to prevent them by taking these simple precautions whenever you leave your car unattended.

- Remove the ignition key.
- Activate the steering lock.
- Shut all windows unless pets or children are inside.
- Remove documents, shopping and other contents or lock them in the boot.
- Lock the car doors, even if leaving the car for only a short time.

Consider taking extra theft-prevention measures:

- Fit an alarm or immobilizing device.
- Have your car's registration number etched on each window.
- When buying new, choose a car that incorporates effective security devices.
- Fit a radio that you can remove and lock in the boot.

THE HIGHWAY CODE SAYS:

- A stolen car can mean having to walk home late at night. It can mean weeks of delay sorting out insurance, extra expense getting into work, loss of personal possessions, and losing your no-claims bonus.

THE MOT TEST

- All motor vehicles three or more years old must have an annual test at a vehicle testing station authorized by the Ministry of Transport. There is a fee for this test.
- Cars passing their test will be issued with an MOT (Ministry of Transport) test certificate. Without it you cannot renew a car's vehicle excise licence.
- When your car's MOT test is due, make an appointment. Allow time for any repairs to be done before the current certificate expires. You may have your vehicle tested one month before the certificate's expiration date.

Tested items

The tester works through a safety checklist:

- steering wheel
- brake pedal travel
- handbrake travel
- bonnet catch security
- horn
- wipers
- brake/clutch fluid level
- seat belts
- glass damage
- reverse lights
- numberplate light
- rear fog lamp
- hazard lights
- spot/fog lamp
- direction indicators
- fuel tank
- brake components
- handbrake cable etc.
- brake lines/hoses
- washers
- headlamp beams
- side lights
- rear lights
- stop lights
- bodywork
- wheels
- tyres
- steering (wear/travel)
- exhausts/mounts
- fuel lines

The MOT test certificate

- If your car passes its test, you will receive an MOT (Ministry of Transport) test certificate showing:
  - Registration mark.
  - Vehicle testing station number.
  - Date of issue.
  - Date of expiry.
  - Serial number of immediately preceding certificate.
  - Vehicle identification or chassis number.
  - Colour.
  - Make.
  - Year of manufacture.
  - Recorded mileage.
  - Design and weight if a goods vehicle.
  - Otherwise, horsepower or engine capacity in cubic centimetres.
  - Tester's signature.
  - Tester's name in block capitals.
  - Authentication stamp.

Failing an MOT

- Cars failing the test must have defects repaired and must be re-tested.
- If your car fails its test and you need to use it, you must first arrange for repairs and a re-test, and make sure these are done.
- Anyone driving a defective vehicle on a road may be prosecuted and their insurance may be invalid.

7. Car systems

A car is a complex piece of machinery. The driving test does not require you to know how it all works, but it is useful to have at least a basic understanding of the main systems involved.

THE CAR BODY

There are three main types of car body (its 'frame').

1 Chassis construction

- This comprises a steel framework onto which the body is bolted. There are three types of chassis: **perimeter**, with a rectangular framework (**a**); **X-frame**, with a strong, deep central spine (**b**); and **space frame**, with many small pieces forming a strong but lightweight construction (**c**).
- Chassis construction permits redesigning the body without reconstructing the whole vehicle. One disadvantage is heaviness; most manufacturers have now turned from chassis to unitary construction.

2 Subframes

- Steel subframes are used in small, transverse-engined cars. The front subframe (**d**) supports the engine and other components. The rear subframe (**e**) supports the rear suspension. The resulting unit is bolted onto the body. Disadvantages include heaviness and corrosion.

3 Unitary construction

- This creates a car body as a pressed-steel shell comprising a ribbed floor pan to which are welded front, rear and side members, supporting the roof.

Robots spot-weld the panels together.
- Unitary construction gives a good power-to-weight ratio, a low-slung body for good aerodynamic performance, and a rigid safety shell around the passengers. Unitary construction also saves manufacturers money.

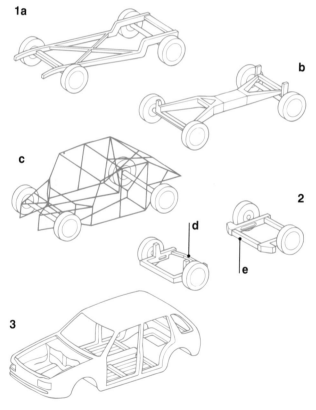

THE ENGINE

Most cars have a petrol engine, but diesel engines have
become increasingly popular.

The petrol engine

● An engine block (**a**) contains cylinders (**b**) with spark
  plugs (**c**) and pistons (**d**) linked to a crankshaft (**e**)
  activated by a starter motor (**f**).

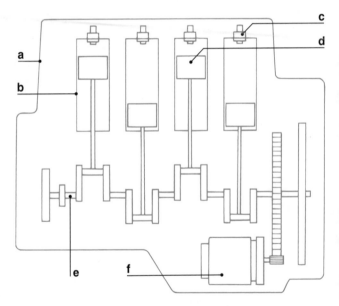

● When you switch on the ignition (**g**), electricity from
  a battery (**h**) activates the starting motor (**f**) which
  turns the crankshaft, making the pistons move up and
  down.

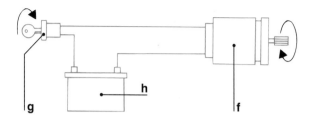

- Current from the battery also flows through a coil boosting the voltage, then to a distributor (**i**) which sets off a spark at each spark plug in turn (**j**).

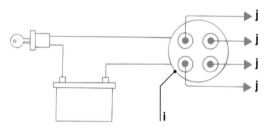

- Meanwhile, the crankshaft works the fuel pump, sending petrol from the petrol tank to the carburettor, where petrol vapour mixes with air. (Some cars use an electric fuel pump.)
- Pressing the accelerator draws the fuel-air mixture into the cylinders.
- Firing in sequence, spark plugs ignite the fuel-air mixture in the cylinders, so that pulses of explosive ignition keep the pistons moving rapidly.
- Connecting rods worked by the pistons now spin the crankshaft fast enough to turn the wheels of the car.

The diesel engine

- This looks much like a petrol engine but works differently. The main difference is that it uses compressed air, not sparks, to make its pistons work.
- A piston (**a**) compresses air (**b**) in a cylinder (**c**).
- Diesel fuel is squirted into the compressed air (**d**).
- Compression has made the air so hot that the fuel-air mixture ignites (**e**) with no need for a spark, pushing the piston back down.

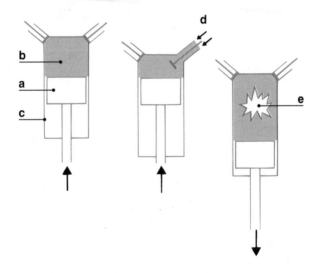

THE ELECTRICAL SYSTEM

Engine, lights, horn and instruments are powered by the battery and the alternator that keeps the battery recharged.

- Turning the ignition switch (**a**) full on sends electric current from the battery (**b**) to the starter motor (**c**).
- The starter motor turns a crankshaft (**d**), setting pistons (**e**) moving to and fro in their cylinders.
- From the battery, electricity also flows to a coil (**f**), which boosts the current's voltage.
- This current goes to the distributor (**g**), which fires spark plugs (**h**) one by one, igniting fuel to drive the pistons and keep the crankshaft turning.
- The turning crankshaft spins a fan belt (**i**) which operates an alternator (**j**) that generates electric current to keep the battery charged.

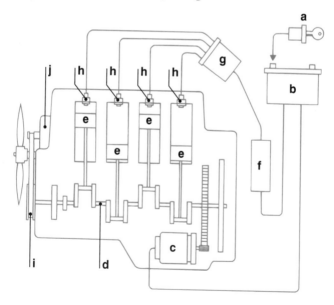

THE TRANSMISSION SYSTEM

This transmits the crankshaft's rotary motion to the wheels by means of a revolving drive shaft and meshing toothed gear wheels. Transmission layout depends on a car's design and whether it has front- or rear-wheel drive.

Rear-wheel drive

● An input shaft (**a**) transmits the drive to the gearbox (**b**), where gears adjust it to the car's speed. A propeller shaft (**c**) then transmits the drive to the rear axle, where crown and pinion gears make two half shafts (**d**) rotate at right angles to the propeller shaft

Rear-wheel drive

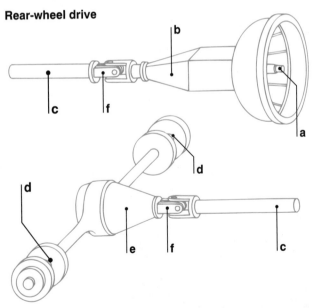

to turn the road wheels. Gears known as the differential (**e**) let the wheels spin at different speeds when rounding a bend. Hinges called universal joints (**f**) let the rear axle rise or fall as its wheels pass over bumps in the road.

Front-wheel drive

● This crams both the gearbox and drive into the engine compartment. There are different transmission layouts for an in-line engine (**a**) and a transverse engine (**b**). The space saved by doing away with the propeller shaft and differential have made front-wheel drive increasingly popular.

Front-wheel drive

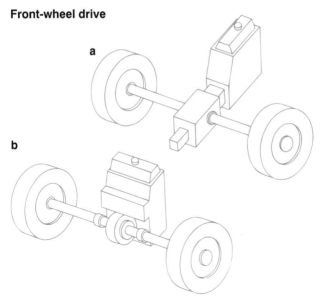

Four-wheel drive

- Used for vehicles such as the Range Rover, this
  transmits the drive to all four road wheels by means
  of a transfer box (**a**) and central differential (**b**). Four-
  wheel drive improves traction, especially on poor
  surfaces, but the system is costly to buy and maintain.
  Some four-wheel drive vehicles used mainly on roads
  can disengage two of the wheels.

Four-wheel drive

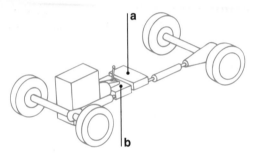

LUBRICATION

A car's engine (**a**), gearbox (**b**), transmission (**c**), final
drive (**d**), suspension (**e**), steering assembly (**f**) and
wheel bearings (**g**) all need lubrication. This protects
moving parts from friction and heat, which can cause
wear or corrosion.

The engine

- Oil under high pressure is pumped around the engine,
  preventing wear on each piston (**h**), cooling the piston
  by transferring heat to the sump (**i**) and, by sealing the
  cylinder, preventing hot gas escaping. So-called

Lubrication points

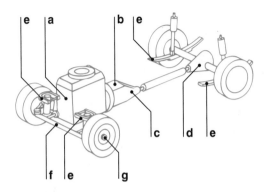

multigrade oils keep a constant level of runniness, or viscosity, whether the engine is cold or hot, and chemical additives improve their performance. British climatic conditions favour the use of SAE 20W–50

Lubrication in engine

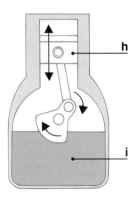

multigrade. Engine oil should be replaced at the intervals prescribed by the manufacturer.

Gearbox and transmission
● Gearboxes and axles tend to be filled with gear oil which is sealed in for life. The gears work in an oil bath or automatically have oil splashed over them as the gearbox is used.

Greasing points
● Sticky grease lubricates moving parts of the transmission, steering, and suspension systems. Joints and bearings may need regular greasing, but in a modern car such components may have grease injected at the factory and sealed in for life. Components subjected to different types of stress will need greases with differing specifications.

COOLING SYSTEMS
When a car burns a fuel-air mixture it produces more heat energy than mechanical energy. Surplus heat must be removed to prevent engine damage. Half the waste heat escapes with the exhaust gases. A cooling system gets rid of the rest.

Water-cooled systems
● A pump (**a**) circulates water or water and antifreeze through holes in the metal water jacket (**b**) surrounding the engine cylinders.
● The liquid coolant carries off excess engine heat through a top hose (**c**) to narrow pipes in a radiator (**d**) cooled by a fan (**e**). From the radiator, heat escapes into the air.

● Then the cooled coolant flows through a bottom hose
  (**f**) back to the water jacket, where reheating occurs.
  In fillable systems, coolant is topped up in the
  radiator by removing its filler cap. (To avoid being
  scalded do this when the engine is cold.)

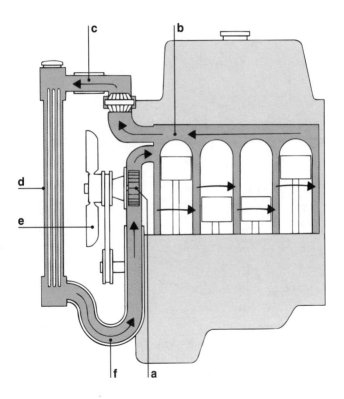

Air-cooled systems

- Deep fins (**a**) help to cool the engine's hottest part by
  enlarging its surface area and encouraging cold air to
  flow over it. An engine-powered fan (**b**) boosts this
  effect.

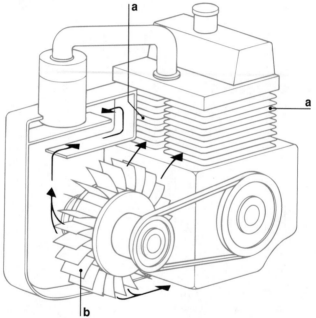

Car heaters

- Water-cooled systems provide special hoses where
  hot coolant heats a small radiator, sending warm air
  into the car's interior.
- Air-cooled engines capture heat from the exhaust
  pipe to warm the inside of the car.

THE STEERING SYSTEM

When you turn the steering wheel this turns the front road wheels, but it does so by acting through gears which help to reduce the driver's effort. There are two main types of system.

Rack and pinion systems

- Turning the steering wheel (**a**) turns the pinion (**b**), a small gear linked to the lower end of the steering column (**c**). The pinion acts on a toothed rack (**d**) mounted across the front of the car. The rack transmits the steering through track rods (**e**) to the road wheels.
- Rack and pinion systems allow precise steering with little effect on the steering wheel.

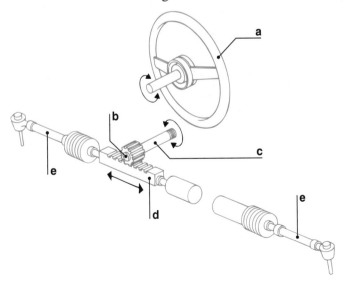

Steering box systems

● A box contains the gear mechanism: a spiral worm
shaft (**a**) at the lower end of the steering column
supporting an internally grooved nut and ball-bearing
assembly (**b**). This assembly travels down or up the
worm shaft as the steering wheel turns, a movement
turning the output shaft (**c**) which emerges from the
steering box. The shaft moves a drop arm (**d**). This
acts on a steering linkage of ball-jointed arms and
track rods which turn the front axles.

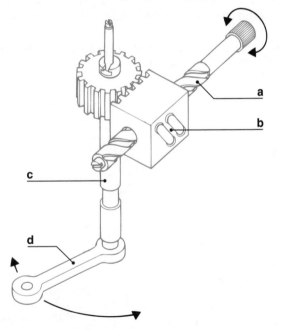

Power-assisted steering

Both types of steering system can come with power-assisted steering, which makes steering easier, requiring less force. Hydraulic fluid pushes a piston which acts on the rack or in the steering box, augmenting the driver's force to reduce the effort needed for turning the steering wheel.

EXHAUST SYSTEMS

These comprise steel pipes through which waste engine gases escape from the back of the car, making way for fresh fuel and air to enter the engine. Special components silence the engine and cut down pollution.

Silencers

These reduce engine noise without unduly affecting performance. There are three main types of silencer.

- **The expansion chamber** is a box (**a**) with inlet (**b**) and outlet (**c**) pipes. As waste gases enter the box, they expand, losing kinetic energy and so some of their noise. They lose more of both on becoming restricted as they enter the outlet pipe.

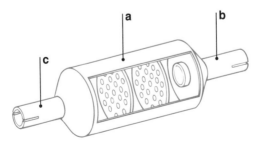

● **The baffle box** is similar to the expansion chamber
  but more effective. It contains a number of staggered
  partitions (**d**), which may be perforated. These cause
  the gases to change direction frequently, so losing
  kinetic energy and noise.

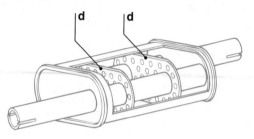

● **The absorption silencer** is a box containing a
  perforated pipe (**e**) surrounded by sound-absorbent
  glass fibre or steel wool (**f**).

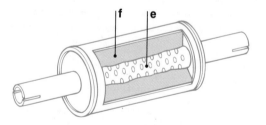

● Most car exhaust systems include several silencers of
  different types, absorbing different sound
  frequencies. Corrosion means that part or all of a
  system may need to be renewed every few years.

Pollution control

Modern cars include devices to makes engines burn
fuel more efficiently, so reducing the amounts of
noxious waste gases emitted through the exhaust
system. In the system itself, there may be a catalytic
converter which changes harmful carbon monoxide and
hydrocarbons into harmless substances.

WHEELS AND TYRES

Road wheels

Besides revolving to keep a car moving, wheels must
be sturdy enough to cope with the stresses imposed by
acceleration, braking, cornering and bumpy roads.

● A typical car wheel comprises a pressed steel disc (**a**)
  welded onto a rim (**b**). The wheel is fixed to a hub by
  pushing the stud holes (**c**) in the wheel disc through
  the three to five threaded studs that jut from the hub
  flange, and using nuts to screw the wheel onto the
  studs.

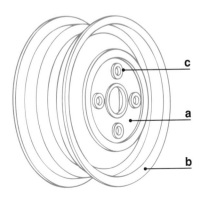

Tyres

These are hollow, reinforced hoops filled with
pressurized air. They fit snugly onto the wheel rims to
cushion the ride. Tyres must also give good grip on the
road and withstand the stresses listed on the
previous page.

- A modern tubeless tyre has no inner tube. It traps air
  between the wheel rim and the tyre's synthetic rubber
  casing. This has sidewalls (**a**), shoulders (**b**), a thick
  outer surface with a deeply grooved, road-gripping
  tread (**c**), and wire-reinforced inner edges or beads
  (**d**) which fit onto the wheel rim. Several layers of
  plies (**e**) made of fabric and steel webbing strengthen
  the casing inside.

Tubeless tyre

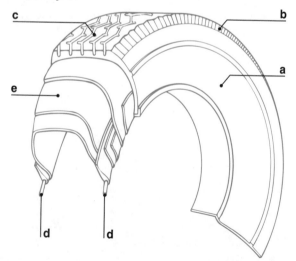

- In cross-ply tyres, the bracing cords of successive plies cross at right angles (**f**).
- In radial tyres, the cords run radially across the tyre (**g**), below a cross-ply breaker belt (**h**) reinforcing the tread.

Radial tyres last longer and give better road holding than cross-ply. It is dangerous (and illegal) to fit both kinds of tyre to the same pair of wheels – front or back.

Cross-ply tyre

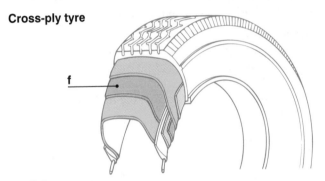

Radial tyre

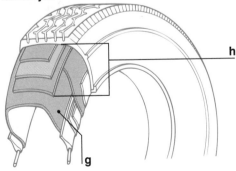

BRAKES

Car brakes work by hydraulic pressure. When the driver presses down on the foot brake, a broad piston in a master cylinder forces brake fluid through slim tubes and against narrower pistons in smaller wheel cylinders. The pressure of this brake fluid pushes these pistons along in their cylinders, making brake shoes or brake pads press on drums or discs, which slow down the road wheels. Many cars have drum brakes on rear wheels and disc brakes on front wheels.

Drum brakes

● These comprise a cast-iron drum (**a**) bolted to the inside of a road wheel, and two semi-circular brake shoes (**b**) lined with heat-resistant material. The drum turns with the road wheel, but the brake shoes do not turn.

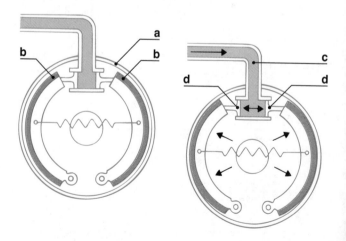

● When the foot brake is pressed, brake fluid (**c**) pushes pistons (**d**) against the brake shoes, which in turn press on the drum. This makes both the drum and its wheel slow down or stop.

Disc brakes

● These comprise a cast-iron disc (**a**) and two metal friction pads (**b**) lined with heat-resistant material, and mounted one on each side of the disc. The disc turns with the road wheel, but the friction pads do not turn.

● When the foot brake is pressed, brake fluid (**c**) pushes pistons (**d**), which force the friction pads to press on the sides of the disc, much as brake shoes pinch the rim of a bicycle wheel. This makes the disc and the road wheel slow down or stop.

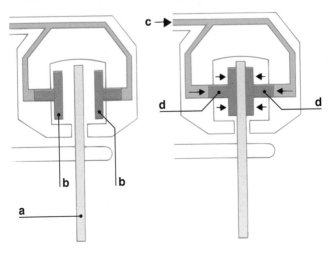

SUSPENSION

Suspension systems help to give a smooth ride over
bumpy surfaces, improve driver control, and reduce
wear and tear on important parts of the car. Some
systems depend on gas or liquid; most involve springs
mounted between the car axles and body. Cars usually
have a separate system for each wheel, so they are said
to have independent suspension.

Coil springs

● A coil spring (**a**) is a flexible metal rod forming a
  spiral that shortens and lengthens as the wheels move
  up and down over bumps in the road. Coil springs
  survive braking and cornering well and are used on
  the front wheels. These springs are a coiled form of a
  type of spring called a torsion bar.

Leaf springs

● A leaf spring (**b**) is simply a stack of steel strips
  called leaves held together and curved up at the ends.

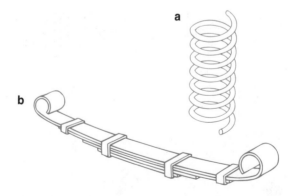

● The ends of the master leaf, the longest, join the car
  body. Leaf springs are most effective when used on
  the rear wheels.

Shock absorbers
● Shock absorbers damp down the action of the springs
  to prevent the car bouncing about. The most common
  shock absorber is the telescopic damper which
  comprises an oil-filled cylinder (**a**) with a piston (**b**).
● When a spring is compressed its damper's piston is
  driven down in the cylinder, forcing oil ahead of it.
  Some slowly escapes (**c**). When a spring is released,
  the piston moves back up (**d**), pushing oil down. By
  retarding the piston, the oil in the damper indirectly
  curbs the spring's up-and-down movements.

Telescopic damper

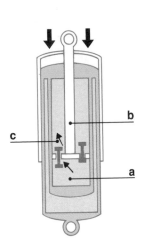
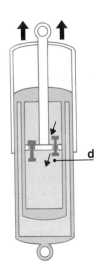

Glossary

acceleration lane A traffic lane where vehicles accelerate before merging with traffic travelling along a dual carriageway or a motorway.

accelerator pedal The driver's right-hand foot pedal. Pressing it boosts the flow of fuel to the engine, increasing the car's power or speed.

alternator A device generating alternating electric current and recharging the battery. It is worked by the crankshaft when the engine is running.

aquaplaning Uncontrolled sliding over a skin of water between tyres and road. A car might aquaplane if driven too fast in wet conditions.

automatic transmission A gear system that works automatically as you increase or reduce pressure on the accelerator pedal. Learners passing a driving test in a car with automatic transmission are only qualified to drive cars with automatic gears. Learners passing their test in cars with manual gears are qualified to drive either type.

battery The device storing electricity to operate the starter motor, produce sparks in the spark plugs, and work the lights, heating, horn, wipers and car radio. The battery is recharged by an alternator or dynamo.

biting point The point at which raising the clutch pedal makes the disengaged clutch plate linked to the car wheels mesh with the plate that is linked to the engine and already revolving.

blind corner A sharp bend where a driver cannot see very far and should proceed slowly enough to be able to stop if the road around the bend is obstructed.

blind spot A part of your field of vision at the side or rear of your car that is obstructed when you look in your mirrors. A brief backward glance should show a vehicle concealed by a blind spot.

box junction A junction with criss-cross yellow road markings. Enter a box junction only if your exit is clear, unless turning right and held up only by oncoming traffic or vehicles waiting to turn right.

brake horsepower (bhp) A measure of engine power.

breathalyzer A device breathed into by a driver to show the level of alcohol in the breath. Police breathalyze motorists suspected of driving after drinking more than the legally permitted amount.

bus lane A traffic lane reserved for buses, and given special signs and road markings. Cars may not enter it except outside any times shown by time plates.

camber A road's convex surface.

carburettor Part of a petrol engine providing the mixture of air and petrol vapour to be burnt inside the cylinders.

catalytic converter A device for converting carbon monoxide and hydrocarbon pollutants into harmless carbon dioxide and water vapour. Car exhaust systems increasingly include these devices.

cat's eyes Reflective glass studs set in the road to show up at night.

cc An engine's cubic capacity. The higher its cc rating, the greater its power.

central reserve Space in the middle of a dual carriageway where vehicles can wait for a gap in the traffic before crossing to the other side. There is also a central reserve down the middle of motorways, but it must not be crossed.

chassis The skeleton supporting the car body in cars not formed (as most now are) as a unitary shell.

choke A valve controlling the amount of air entering the carburettor. Partly closing this valve reduces the air intake, making a cold engine easy to start.

clearway A stretch of road where you may stop only if in a traffic queue, if you break down, or in an emergency.

clutch The device connecting and disconnecting the engine from the wheels while you change gear.

clutch slip Raising the clutch pedal to the biting point where both clutch plates are partly engaged, and the plate spun by the engine begins to turn the plate linked to the wheels.

coasting Travelling in neutral or with the clutch kept pressed down. Coasting is illegal because a coasting car is not fully under control.

contraflow system A traffic flow system (at some roadworks on motorways, for example) where you must drive in a traffic lane normally used for oncoming vehicles.

controlled crossing A crossing controlled by an authorized person or by traffic signals.

crankshaft A device in the engine which converts the pistons' reciprocating (to and fro) motion into the rotary motion which turns the wheels.

cutting in After overtaking, pulling in so sharply that the overtaken vehicle is forced to slow down or change direction. You should overtake fast enough to pull in quickly without this happening.

deceleration Reducing speed by letting the accelerator pedal rise rather than braking. A preliminary brief touch on the foot brake would warn following vehicles that you are slowing down.

deceleration lane A traffic lane for vehicles slowing down as they start to leave a dual carriageway or a motorway.

diesel engine An internal combustion engine that uses diesel oil instead of petrol for fuel.

dipstick A metal stick that slots into a hole in the engine casing. If removed, wiped clean, reinserted, and removed again, it shows whether the oil level is high or low. The level is topped up by unscrewing a cap on the engine casing and pouring oil into the hole.

dipswitch The switch dipping your headlamps. Drivers should dip their headlamps while meeting or following another vehicle.

double white lines These lines along the centre of a road forbid overtaking where this is hazardous.

driving licence A licence permitting someone to drive one or more categories of vehicle. Holders of a provisional licence may drive only while supervised.

dual carriageway A broad road with two or more traffic lanes in each direction, and a central reserve.

emergency vehicles These include police cars, fire engines, ambulances, and bomb disposal, blood transfusion and coastguard vehicles – all with blue flashing beacons. Drivers should move out of their way quickly but safely, and should also give way to doctors' vehicles with green flashing beacons.

flooding the engine Keeping a choke out too long so that the engine is flooded with petrol and stalls.

foot brake The middle floor-mounted pedal in front of the driver. Pressing it forces fluid through pipes to cylinders on the wheels, pushing shoes or pads against drums or discs to make the wheels stop or slow down.

gear lever The usually floor-mounted lever moved forward, back and sideways to change gear. In some cars the gear lever projects from the steering column or instrument panel.

gears Cogwheels of different sizes borne on two shafts in a gearbox – one spun by the engine, the other making the road wheels revolve. Changing gear makes different cogwheels interlock, varying the ratio of the speed between engine and road wheels.

handbrake The hand-operated, usually floor-mounted lever applied for parking and whenever a car is stopped for more than a moment or two. In some cars the handbrake is situated below the instrument panel.

hard shoulder The hard-surfaced strip to the left of the left-hand traffic lane of a motorway. Drivers may stop on it only in an emergency, and must not drive along it except where special signs tell them to, as where roadworks have closed one or more traffic lanes.

hatch or herringbone markings These road markings may bracket a reserve area at a junction on a main road. Drivers on the main road may not cross the markings except to enter the reserve area before turning right, and then not if the hatch markings are edged by a continuous white line.

hazard Anything that could make a driver alter speed or direction. Hazards include roadworks, obstacles in the road, pedestrians, oncoming vehicles, and junctions and roundabouts.

hazard warning lights Paired flashing lights at the front, rear and sides of a vehicle. Use them to warn other vehicles if you have broken down.

Highway Code A set of rules essential for every road user to follow. Not all are laid down as law, but disregarding any might make conviction more likely for someone charged with a motoring offence.

insurance Car drivers are legally obliged to take out third-party insurance against causing injury or damage to other people or their property.

jack A tool that slots into a jacking point under a vehicle and can be screwed up to raise the wheels of one side clear of the ground for tyre changing.

jump leads Two insulated wires which can be attached to two batteries to recharge one from the other.

lighting-up time The time after which headlamps must be on except in a built-up area that has street lamps at intervals of less than 185 m (202 yd).

mini-roundabout A small roundabout in the middle of a normal road junction. Vehicles must circulate clockwise around it.

MOT certificate A certificate granted to a vehicle over a certain age when it passes the Ministry of Transport's annual roadworthiness test.

motorway A fast, multi-lane highway with a maximum speed of 70 mph and no stopping permitted, except on the hard shoulder in an emergency. Learner drivers may not use motorways.

nearside In the UK, the left-hand side of a vehicle as viewed from behind.

odometer The instrument showing a vehicle's current and accumulated mileage.

offside In the UK, the right-hand side of a vehicle as viewed from behind.

one-way street A street along which all traffic must move in the same direction.

pelican crossing A pedestrian crossing with pedestrian-controlled lights that go from red to flashing amber to green. Drivers must stop on red and give way to pedestrians when the amber light is flashing.

puffin crossing A pedestrian-controlled crossing with lights that go green automatically after a pedestrian has crossed the road.

road excise licence An annual licence to use a vehicle on a public road. Licensed vehicles are given a tax disc, which must be displayed low in the nearside corner of the windscreen, facing forward.

road markings These are markings, along or across the carriageway, or on the kerb or edge. They include stop lines, lines that forbid overtaking, and lines showing parking restrictions.

skidding Sliding, as when slamming the brakes on too hard locks the wheels so that the tyres lose their grip on the road. The risk of skidding is high if you brake sharply at high speed or on ice.

slipping the clutch See CLUTCH SLIP.

slip road The roads leading to and from a motorway. See ACCELERATION LANE and DECELERATION LANE.

spark plug A plug producing an electric spark which ignites the air-fuel mixture in a cylinder in the car engine.

speed limit The maximum legally permitted speed. This is 70 mph on dual carriageways and motorways, and 60 mph on all other roads. Lower limits apply in built-up areas and with certain conditions, such as roadworks.

stalling Stopping the car's engine by accident, as when too much use of the choke floods the engine.

tailgating Following closely behind another vehicle: a risky practice that should be avoided.

tax disc See ROAD EXCISE LICENCE.

three-point turn Reversing a car in a road by making a three-stage manoeuvre: forward, turning; backward, turning; then forward again, turning and straightening out.

traffic lane Part of a road carrying traffic proceeding in one direction. A one-way street usually has at least two traffic lanes. A dual carriageway has at least two in each direction. A motorway can have more than four.

traffic signals These are lights used to control junctions, roadworks, narrow bridges, and crossings for pedestrians, trains and trams. They also operate outside fire stations and ambulance stations.

traffic signs These are pictorial or verbal signs on posts or gantries. They order, warn, direct or inform.

two-second rule The rule that says in good driving conditions you should keep at least a two-second safety gap between your vehicle and the one ahead. In poor conditions the gap should be much greater.

tyres These should be of matching type, and checked regularly to make sure they are properly inflated and have the minimum legal tread depth.

unleaded petrol Petrol without a lead additive. Unleaded petrol is environmentally safer than leaded petrol as lead from vehicle exhausts can impair the health of people living near busy roads.

U-turn Reversing a car in the road by a single manoeuvre. U-turns are forbidden in some roads and dangerous in all except wide, quiet streets.

zebra crossing This pedestrian crossing has black-and-white stripes across the road, flashing yellow beacons on each side, warning zig-zag approach lines, and give-way lines where drivers must stop to let pedestrians across.

Index

COLLINS POCKET REFERENCE

COLLINS POCKET REFERENCE

Weddings
An invaluable guide to all wedding arrangements,
from the engagement to the honeymoon

Scottish Surnames
A guide to the family names of Scotland

(All above titles £4.99)

Clans and Tartans
The histories and tartans of over 130 clans

(£6.99)